Y0-BCS-401

Our God Is Undocumented

Our God Is Undocumented

Biblical Faith and Immigrant Justice

Ched Myers and Matthew Colwell

ORBIS BOOKS
Maryknoll, New York 10545

BV
4647
.H67
M94
2012

Founded in 1970, Orbis Books endeavors to publish works that enlighten the mind, nourish the spirit, and challenge the conscience. The publishing arm of the Maryknoll Fathers and Brothers, Orbis seeks to explore the global dimensions of the Christian faith and mission, to invite dialogue with diverse cultures and religious traditions, and to serve the cause of reconciliation and peace. The books published reflect the views of their authors and do not represent the official position of the Maryknoll Society. To learn more about Maryknoll and Orbis Books, please visit our website atwww.maryknollsociety.org.

Copyright © 2012 by Ched Myers and Matthew Colwell

Published by Orbis Books, Box 302, Maryknoll, NY 10545-0302.

All rights reserved.

No part of this publication may be reproduced or transmitted in any form or by any means, electronic or mechanical, including photocopying, recording, or any information storage or retrieval system, without prior permission in writing from the publisher.

Queries regarding rights and permissions should be addressed to: Orbis Books, P.O. Box 302, Maryknoll, NY 10545-0302.

Manufactured in the United States of America

Library of Congress Cataloging-in-Publication Data

Myers, Ched.
    Our God is undocumented: biblical faith and immigrant justice / Ched Myers and Matthew Colwell.
    p. cm.
    Includes bibliographical references.
    ISBN 978-1-57075-956-7 (pbk.); eISBN 978-1-60833-115-4
    1. Hospitality—Religious aspects—Christianity.   2. Hospitality—Biblical teaching.
3. Hospitality—United States.   4. Emigration and immigration—Religious aspects—
Christianity.   5. Emigration and immigration in the Bible.   6. United States—
Emigration and immigration.   I. Colwell, Matthew.   II. Title.
BV4647.H67M94 2012
 261.7—dc23

                                                                          2011035441

To Roberto and Yolanda Martinez
and Gloria and Ross Kinsler,

elders, teachers, and mentors in the struggle for human rights
and biblical justice

Contents

Acknowledgments

This project has been many years in the making. We are grateful to Orbis Books for its interest in publishing it and trust that it will be of use in the ongoing struggle for immigrant rights in the United States and beyond.

Both of us have been deeply impacted by the many faces and stories of the immigrant poor we have encountered in the course of our lives and ministries. Colleagues who have also inspired Matt's thinking on immigration include Rick Ufford-Chase, Ron Garton, Ricardo Moreno, and the five activists featured in this book. Ched has been mentored over the last quarter century by veterans of immigrant rights work such as David Burciaga, Fr. Luis Olivares, Walden Bello, Demetria Martinez, Domingo Gonzalez, Ron Fujiyoshi, Aurora Camacho de Schmidt, Orlando Tizon, Maria Jimenez, Pablo Alvarado, and Alexia Salvatierra. We are also grateful to our partners, Jill and Elaine, for their patience and support over the course of this project.

We have dedicated this book to two couples who have, in different ways, embodied the argument of this volume. Ross and Gloria Kinsler were Presbyterian missionaries in Central America for thirty-five years, deeply involved in liberation theology and solidarity work. The late Roberto Martinez (1937–2009), who Matt profiles in Chapter 10, and his wife Yolanda were colleagues of Ched's for many years with the American Friends Service Committee, exemplary and legendary activists in the borderlands. The first copy of this book will be presented to the Roberto Martinez Memorial Library at Friends Center in San Diego, dedicated in July 2011. We live in gratitude for their work and witness.

Introduction

Church without Borders

Ched Myers

> *Christ is our peace; in his body he has made two
> groups into one and has broken down the dividing
> wall which is the hostility between us. (Eph 2:14)*

On June 1, 2008, two San Diego area ministers led a
binational prayer vigil and "Lovefeast" (in the Moravian tradition) at the U.S.-Mexico border fence at Friendship Park.
Methodist John Fanestil and Nazarene Jamie Gates passed
sweetbread and tamarindo juice through the fence to the
Tijuana side in an effort to demonstrate Christian solidarity
across borders. They and others then began weekly Sunday
communion services at the fence (see Fanestil 2008).

On February 21, 2009, Gates and Fanestil called for a
major worship service, with "congregations" on both sides
of the fence, including a cross-border choir singing Gabriel
Faure's *Requiem*. This time some 150 participants on the
U.S. side were surrounded by media, loud anti-immigrant
counterprotestors and an unprecedented show of force by
San Diego police, State Park Rangers, Coast Guard, and
Border Patrol officers. For the first time during this campaign, however, a phalanx of heavily armed Border Patrol
agents prevented the ministers from approaching the fence

to serve communion. After serving the congregants on the U.S. side, Fanestil turned toward the fence to attend to those on the Mexican side. Border Patrol agents raised their weapons and gave warning, then arrested, handcuffed, and detained Fanestil.

This experiment in a public liturgy of resistance and reconciliation stands in a deep biblical tradition. For example, the Epistle to the Ephesians portrays the Apostle Paul as a prisoner (Eph 3:1–3) because of his commitment to the "mystery" of God's dream of the "re-unification of all things" (1:9–10). At the heart of this mystery is the cosmic impact of Christ's death on the cross, through which the Apostle claims that *all* walls of division have been broken down, and all laws legitimating enmity have been nullified (2:14–16).

In Hellenistic antiquity the cultural, economic, and political conflict between Jew and Gentile was considered to be the prototype of all human hostility. The gospel of Ephesians, however, asserts that Christ has forged "in his body" a new social solidarity between these alienated peoples, which is specifically articulated in terms of a grant of "citizenship":

Eph 2:12: "you [Gentiles] were . . . excluded from citizenship (Gk *politeias*) in Israel and strangers (Gk *xenoi*) to the covenants of promise."

2:19: "you are no longer foreigners (Gk *xenoi*) and strangers but are fellow citizens (Gk *sumpolitai*)…"

This radical principle of "open borders" would have been profoundly challenging for both groups. For Jews, an ethnic minority already struggling against the forces of assimilation in the dominating culture of the Roman Empire, the prospect of welcoming their historic enemies into their tradition on equal footing was utterly counterintuitive. Conversely, Roman citizens would hardly have aspired to join a marginalized and oppressed people who didn't even have their own national sovereignty! Yet this was the summons of Ephesians: to build this inconceivable bridge "on Christ's back."

According to the epistle, Christ's cross has enabled the construction of a new "house without walls," articulated in 2:19–22 (note the repetitive use of the Greek root *oiko*):

> So then you are no longer foreigners and strangers (literally "outside the house," Gk *paroikoi*), but are fellow citizens with the saints and members of the household (*oikeioi*) of God, built upon (*epoikodomē thentes*) the foundation of the apostles and prophets, with Christ Jesus himself as the "keystone." The whole structure (*oikodomē*) is joined together in Christ and grows into a holy Temple in the Lord, in whom you also are built (*sunoikodomeisthe*) into it for a dwelling place (*katoikētērion*) of God in the Spirit.

This undivided house is not architectural at all, but an organic, *human* entity, joined sinew to sinew and heart to heart (see 4:16).

Ephesians wreaks havoc on ideologies of xenophobia and exclusion, then and now (for a more detailed exposition, see Myers and Enns 2009, 82ff). The 2008–09 communion services at the border fence faithfully exegeted and embodied this vision by trying to realize "church without borders." Indeed, Ephesians goes on to say that because

Christ has deconstructed our ideologies of nationhood and ethnic segregation, the church's proper vocation is to proclaim this mystery to the highest authorities (Eph 3:9–10). Pursuing this vocation in a world of division inevitably entails challenging statutory laws, cultural prejudices, and institutionalized separations (2:15), as did the "transgressive communion" of Rev. Fanestil and the congregants at the heart of the U.S.-Mexico border war zone. Because Christ has declared *shalom* "to those far off and to those near" (2:13, 17), the church should not live peaceably with walls of hostility.

★   ★   ★

This book offers various perspectives on the problems and prospects of becoming a "church without borders." The last five years have seen a number of helpful books published on the topic of the faith community and contemporary issues of immigration in the United States.[1] Our aim is to supplement, but not duplicate, these studies. *Our God Is Undocumented* (the title is explained in Chapter 3) is an unapologetically theological and ecclesial reflection on "migrant ministry" in the North American context. As suggested by the opening meditation above, our perspective is informed in equal parts by ancient word and contemporary deed.

The odd-numbered essays herein are my biblical reflections on issues germane to the moral terrain of the immigration question, such as cultural diversity (Chapter 1), hospitality (Chapter 3), God's vision of inclusiveness (Chapter 5), embracing "otherness" (Chapter 7), and welcoming the refugee (Chapter 9). The even-numbered chapters are Matt Colwell's profiles of women and men who we regard as exemplary practitioners of immigrant justice: two white

North American ministers (Chapters 2 and 8), two Salvadoran activists (Chapters 4 and 6), and a recently deceased Chicano human rights organizer (Chapter 10). This "bifocal" approach is grounded in the conviction that Bible study and practical discipleship help interpret each other and that both are crucial to our spiritual, moral, and political formation.[2]

Word. Torah and the Prophets warned Israel not to discriminate against economic or political refugees, since in YHWH's eyes even the chosen people were "but aliens and tenants" (Lv 25:23). Instead, they were to treat the "sojourners in your midst" with dignity and justice (Dt 24:14). This fundamental regard for the resident alien, and call to solidarity with the "outsider," came to full realization in the teaching and practice of Jesus of Nazareth. An oft-cited verse that captures this is Matthew's last-judgment parable, in which Jesus commends those who welcome him in the guise of a stranger—and condemns those who do not (Mt 25:35–46). The biblical essays in this book, however, explore beyond such well-known terrain, examining powerful texts from each Testament that are rarely considered in the immigration debate. In various ways they express the divine mandate to include "outsiders" in the circle of justice and human rights.

Deed. Our biblical tradition, though strong and enduring, has a crucial vulnerability: its credibility depends upon people willing to "make the Word flesh." This is why we have devoted half this book to the testimonies of contemporary immigrant rights organizers. Each of the five persons profiled is a friend and colleague from whom Matt and I have learned a great deal. Some are immigrants themselves, some are clergy, and all are activists of deep faith and clear politics who have demonstrated extraordinary creativity and persistence in their work. Their discipleship (and citizenship) is exemplary, and in the tradition of what my mentor James McClendon (2002) called "biography as theology," we are honored to share their stories.

★   ★   ★

Issues related to the geopolitical definition of human communities, to the continuing and often involuntary migration of peoples, and to the social problems that result from the displacement and relocation of immigrants, are complex in our modern global civilization and deserve careful reflection and deliberation. And there are many sound sociological and political arguments (and statistical evidence) for why immigration represents a net gain to North American society, and why democratic citizens should support immigrant justice. But for Christians, these issues are finally theological, ecclesial, and pastoral. Consequently, this book is more concerned with the deeper moorings for a faith-rooted ethic regarding the "sojourner" in our midst than with the current debates over U.S. immigration and naturalization policies.

Policy advocacy is important, of course. I first became involved in such work in the wake of the Immigration Reform and Control Act of 1986. Now, a quarter century later, the U.S. government again seeks "comprehensive immigration reform," and in Appendix I, Allison Johnson, former coordinator of Christians for Comprehensive Immigration Reform, gives a brief overview of this terrain. Our own policy concerns—including immigrant criminalization, family reunification, amnesty, and asylum—are woven throughout these chapters, and it is our hope that these essays might contribute to the current (and ever more sharply polarized) public conversation. Our *primary* aim here, however, is to look past the heated rhetoric of the day, and to instead reflect on what it means for Christian disciples to be faithful to an "undocumented" God and a "refugee Christ" (Chapter 9).

We are not (and this volume is not) "neutral" when it comes to the current culture war raging around immigration. We are firmly committed to the deepest biblical traditions of, and to current expressions of, immigrant justice and "prophetic hospitality" (see Chapter 3). This bias arises from our own experiences with immigrants as well as from our study of scripture. Both have taught us that God has a special relationship with those marginalized by social and political systems and therefore that the church should as well. One of Jesus' most inappropriately quoted and misunderstood sayings is that "the poor will always be with you" (Mk14:7). As an isolated text it is notoriously (and often cynically) deployed by politicians and preachers alike to excuse or minimize the existence of poverty, as if Jesus was stipulating its inevitability as a condition of nature or, worse, as part of the divine plan. In fact, Jesus' statement was identifying the true social location of the church. "*You,*" he told the disciples emphatically, "will always be *with the poor.*"[3] And immigrants, particularly the undocumented, are arguably the poorest and most vulnerable population in North America today.

Jesus understood that our *perspectives* on marginalized people are determined by our *proximity* to them. Tragically, most of our churches exhibit little proximity to the immigrant poor, though they are everywhere in our midst. Matt and I write self-consciously as members of these churches, in hopes of encouraging and challenging them to deeper involvement.

I first met Matt as a serious and engaged student at Fuller Theological Seminary. He subsequently did two stints with us at Bartimaeus Cooperative Ministries and provided the original idea and energy for this book. Matt is currently a Presbyterian pastor in Pasadena who has been active in living wage campaigns, the New Sanctuary Movement, and recent efforts to oppose free trade agreements with Colombia and Honduras. He first became interested in immigration issues by leading U.S. mission teams of mutual learning and service hosted by Presbyterian Border Ministries. During these trips to work with Mexican churches in Agua Prieta, Mexicali, and Tijuana, Matt's consciousness was raised about the complex forces that impacted immigration. He was further moved by his conversations at Casa del Migrante in Tijuana with migrants about the desperate circumstances they faced, by the crosses attached to the border wall that commemorate the hundreds who have died crossing north, and by the 2002 Word and World school on the theme of borderlands justice in Tucson. His five profiles below are based on interviews he conducted in 2008 as part of his Doctor of Ministry project at San Francisco Theological Seminary.

I am a Mennonite social justice theologian and popular educator, now based in Ventura County. I was introduced to immigration issues in the early 1980s while working with indigenous peoples movements in the Pacific Basin and with the Sanctuary Movement. During my tenure with the American Friends Service Committee in the Pacific Southwest between 1987 and 1997, I was intimately involved with immigrant rights work at the local (organizing day laborers), regional (documenting human rights abuses along Southwest borderlands) and national levels (policy advocacy and education). Most of the perspectives expressed in my essays below were developed during that period, and my wife Elaine and I continue to be shaped by our relationships with immigrant families in East Los Angeles. In recent years I have supported the work of Clergy and Laity United for Economic Justice in southern California and Interfaith Worker Justice nationally. Underneath all this is a psychic legacy of immigration, assimilation, and conflicted identity that resides in my bones; I have reflected upon this briefly in the Afterword.

We write from our common and distinctive geopolitical vantage point; I am a fifth-generation Californian; Matt is second generation. The American Southwest is the "front line" in the struggle over immigration, and we intentionally chose to profile activists who are organizing in this context. As middle-class, educated white males, we do not pretend to speak "for" immigrants—only to stand with them. The primary purpose of this book is to challenge North American churches with a degree of social power to greater political imagination and response-ability (see Chapters 2 and 8). The question driving our approach here is not *whether* Christians should be involved in immigrant solidarity, but rather *how* and *why*.

★   ★   ★

A theological approach to immigration can only be done with critical awareness of the social, historical, and political context of the presenting issues. Too much of the public discourse today focuses on symptomatic "problems," without understanding their causes, particularly the "push" and "pull" of global economic and political forces that drive immigration, past and present. If our churches are to live in solidarity with the immigrant poor, we must understand the larger structural forces that first displace them.

There are, in our opinion, two major problems in most current public discussions about "illegal immigration." The first is lack of historical perspective. We should never forget that the first immigration "crisis" on this continent came as a result of European colonization of the Americas. This resulted in three great disasters: the obliteration of First Nations, sovereignty and cultures, the violent removal of millions of Africans to the Americas in the slave trade, and the impoverishment of countless people due to relentless resource and labor extraction. As Cuban émigré Miguel de la Torre (2009) likes to remind us, poor immigrants today are simply following the trail of wealth stolen from their land centuries ago.

Subsequent U.S. history has been a narrative of continental conquest resulting in shifting borders and immigrant ebb and flow in response to economic boom and bust. The nineteenth-century ideology of Manifest Destiny, which still shapes our modern imperial mindset (see Williams 1980), first functioned between 1820 and 1850 to justify the nullification of both Mexican and Indian territorial integrity during the westward expansion of more than four million white Americans (see Chacon and Davis 2006). The Treaty of Guadalupe Hidalgo that ended the Mexican-American War of 1846–48 ceded some 40 percent of Mexico's land to the United States, including California, Arizona, New Mexico, Nevada, Utah, Colorado, and parts of Wyoming and Oklahoma. This left more than 125,000 Mexicans residing in territories "crossed" by a border that had suddenly moved north. With the Federal Land Act of 1851, many Mexican holdings in the United States were nullified as well, and the Gadsden Purchase of 1853 added further Mexican territory. Massive deportations followed, in which people of Mexican descent (or those who appeared so), regardless of how many generations they had lived on their land, were sent south in trainloads (see Ufford-Chase 2005). This history did not end with the establishment of the fifty states (including the duplicitous annexation of the independent nation of Hawai'i), but has continued through countless neocolonial interventions, from the Caribbean to the Philippines to the Middle East today.

A second problem in the current debate is the typical emphasis on "pull" rather than "push" factors in immigration, which invariably caricatures third-world migrants as opportunistically taking advantage of better social and economic conditions in the United States. This is certainly true for many legal immigrants today—as it was for the ancestors of most European Americans! However, the vast majority of undocumented immigrants are here as part of a struggle to survive having been *involuntarily* pushed from their homelands and/or livelihoods by military, political, and economic forces beyond their control.

War and foreign interventions have been and continue to be one major "push" factor. One can trace immigration patterns over the last half century directly to the impact of U.S. policies toward "sending" countries. For example, political scientist Saskia Sassen (1988) points out that in the five years before the 1965 U.S. military intervention in the Dominican Republic, some five thousand Dominicans emigrated to the United States; in the five years following, the number increased to some sixty thousand. The war in

Indochina brought tens of thousands of Southeast Asians as refugees. Likewise, another decade of U.S.-sponsored counterinsurgency warfare in the 1980s in Central America brought hundreds of thousands of Salvadorans, Nicaraguans, and Guatemalans (see Chapters 4 and 6). And over the last twenty years, U.S. interventions in the Arab world have increased those populations here.

Economic policies have had similar impact. For example, in the early twentieth century, foreign investors and the Mexican landlord class promoted the state-sponsored disintegration of communal landholdings in Mexico. "By the 1920's, U.S. interest controlled 80 percent of Mexican roads, 81 percent of the mining industry's total capital, and 61 percent of total investment in the oil fields" (Chacon and Davis 2006, 104). Such economic imperialism brought on the Mexican Revolution of 1910–20, which along with the displacement of millions of small farmers, drove many Mexicans north to the United States. More recently, the same patterns have followed policies of international "structural adjustment," export-led development and "modernization." The United States collaborated with national security states in Asia to promote rapid industrialization in the 1980s, spawning not only repression in places like South Korea and the Philippines, but also many economic refugees who ended up in sweatshops and factories in our cities.

Neoliberal deregulation, privatization, and free trade policies have functioned to disrupt or destroy countless third-world communities of small landholders and subsistence farmers (see Brubaker 2007). The North American Free Trade Agreement 1994 (NAFTA) is a dramatic case in point. As U.S. capital flowed into Mexico, the *ejido* system (the product of land reform after the Mexican Revolution) was further dismantled to make way for foreign corporate-controlled agriculture for export. This disenfranchised and displaced countless Mexican *campesinos* (see Bacon 2004). In the very same year, the Clinton administration inaugurated "Operation Gatekeeper," an intensified militarization of the U.S.-Mexico border, in an attempt to stem the very tide of undocumented immigration created by NAFTA (see Nevins 2010; Chacon and Davis 2006).

During this same period, U.S. industrial flight to third-world "free export zones" was netting prosperity for elites in host countries but social disruption for workers. The "pull" of jobs in Mexican *maquiladoras*, for example, uprooted young women from village life, destroying the traditional social fabric and intensifying rural poverty, while creating new dysfunctional "company towns" at the border (see Peña 1997). Sassen (1988) concludes that foreign investment and export-oriented economic development, commonly thought to deter immigration, have had the opposite effect, as newly industrializing countries are the major source of immigrants to the United States.

In fact, fluctuations in domestic U.S. immigration policy throughout history have always been determined by economic forces. During the railroad boom of the 1860s and 1870s, Chinese contract laborers were actively recruited. But in 1882, as the "railroad bubble" was bursting (causing the Panic of 1883), the Chinese Exclusion law was passed. This was one of the most restrictive immigration legislations in U.S. history (and included political bans on anarchists and Communists). Similarly, Mexican workers were actively sought due to a World War I labor shortage; a half million workers were then deported during the Depression of the 1930s. Mexican agricultural workers were again recruited during World War II through the *bracero* program, only to be deported in the Eisenhower administration's "Operation Wetback."

This economic pendulum sends a perpetual double message to immigrant labor: "We need you but we don't want you." With U.S. economic stagnation in the 1980s, immigrant scapegoating grew predictably, reaching fever pitch just as double-dip recession peaked in California. This was accompanied by a rise in hate crimes and reactionary nativist activism, culminating in 1994's Proposition 187. The same trends are evident today in the wake of the financial industry's meltdown and the most significant economic depression since the 1930s. "There is an unmistakable pattern to recession in the United States," wrote sociologist Jorge Bustamante (1992); "when unemployment rises beyond politically acceptable levels, xenophobic sentiments go on the march."

The real tragedy is that a global economy that keeps displacing peoples and U.S. policies that promote the free movement of capital but restrict movements of labor make the widespread frustration about immigration inevitable. Deindustrialization in the United States, and the resulting casualization of labor in an increasingly service-oriented and even "underground" economy, will continue to "pull" immigrant labor and economic refugees.[4] Criminalizing undocumented immigration is particularly duplicitous in light of the fact that the low wage sectors of our economy are utterly dependent upon their labor. Those who wish to address these symptoms, therefore, would do better to work to close the global "open shop" than our southern border.

If we are going to talk about how undocumented immigrants impact *our* society, we ought to first address how our national policies have disrupted *their* lives. Above all, solidarity with the immigrant poor should seek to know them not as statistics, but as human beings who endure extraordinary hardship and trauma in their struggle just to survive—especially since the structural causes of their impoverishment lie on *our* side of the border.

★   ★   ★

Finally, we have a pastoral concern about our fractured identity as predominately a "nation of immigrants." Ever since Columbus, European conquerors and settlers of the Americas have justified their entitlement to the land and its fruits through myths that asserted a divine right to migrate in search of freedom and opportunity. Once entrenched, however, they have often turned around and, through complementing myths of proprietary nationhood, restricted or denied that "right" to newer (and ethnically different) immigrant groups. "Over the past two centuries," writes Sassen, "each new wave of immigrants has encountered strenuous opposition from earlier arrivals."

But living in wholesale (if convenient) denial of our past is unacceptable for people of biblical faith. It was Israel's own bitter experience of displacement that undergirded its ethic of just compassion toward outsiders: "You shall not wrong or oppress a resident alien, for you were aliens in the land of Egypt" (Ex 22:21). As a pastoral task, therefore, it could not be more important for churches to help their members work through their conflicted identities as immigrant peoples. I have explored this briefly below (Chapter 3), and Appendix II offers a simple model for how Christians might talk about recovering their cultural history. Such work is crucial to what Dr. Martin Luther King, Jr. called the "struggle for the soul of America."

Jose Marti, a Cuban patriot of the late nineteenth century who was a vigorous critic of U.S. imperialism, was nevertheless thrilled by the dedication of the Statue of Liberty on the occasion of the first U.S. centenary in 1876. The remarkable inscription from immigrant poet Emma Lazarus ("Give me your tired, your poor, your huddled masses yearning to breathe free. . . . Send those, the homeless, tempest-tossed to me, I lift my lamp beside the Golden Door") suggested to Marti a great counterpoint to U.S. imperial ethnocentrism. As long as that statue stands, the tradition of immigrant hospitality and justice it symbolizes will continue to haunt us. Will we whose ancestors respected no boundaries seek to erect impermeable borders? Will the descendants of Ellis Island bar the "golden door" (see Chapter 9), even as our economic and military policies around the globe continue to create "tempest-tossed" populations? Or will we listen, as did pastors Fanestil and Gates at Friendship Park, to the voice of Christ speaking through the immigrant poor: "Listen! I stand at the door, knocking; if you hear my voice and open the door, I will come in to you and we will share communion" (Rv 3:20).

The integrity of our churches, and the viability of our body politic, depend upon how we answer these questions. Matt and I pray that the inspiration of the following testimonies from both scripture and contemporary practitioners will help to animate more courageous and compassionate experiments in becoming "church without borders."

Chapter 1

Cultural Diversity and Deep Social Ecology:
Genesis 11 and Acts 2

Ched Myers

*How is it that we heard, each of us, in our
own native tongue? (Acts 2:8)*

Southern California today is one of the most multicultural metropolises in the world. Latinos are now (again!) a majority, according to the most recent census. But the diversity of this place is as old as it is contemporary. Prior to European colonization, this land was populated by widely heterogeneous peoples. The various indigenous tribes used different linguistic systems, and while there was rich cultural and economic interaction between them, no one tribe exercised hegemony. And of the original twenty-two members of the Spanish colonizing expedition that came up from northern Mexico in 1781 to establish Los Angeles, there were eight mulattos, eight Indians, two blacks, one mestizo, and only three Spaniards! So from the beginning, our place has been distinctively *multicultural*.

This is important because in the United States today we are still socialized to believe that cultural diversity is a dubious modern development to be feared, not a deep past to be learned from. Yet our local demographic trends represent the future of the United States as a whole; we are *already* being transformed, regardless of whether or not we wish to be a multicultural society. The question facing us is only how we will adjust to this new/old reality.

"It is impossible to say to which human family we belong," the Venezuelan nationalist Simon Bolivar wrote about the Americas in 1819. "Europeans have mixed with the Indians and the Negroes, and Negroes have mixed with the Indians; we were all born of one mother America, though our fathers had different origins." Bolivar's vision, however, stands in sharp contrast to the subsequent observation of French statesman Alexis de Tocqueville in *Democracy in America* (1835): "The European is to the other races of mankind what man himself is to the lower animals: he makes them subservient to his use and when he cannot subdue them he destroys them." In fact, the Americas have always been defined by the struggle between dominant culture ideologies of conformity imposed by those in power, and grassroots cultural diversity among those on the margins.

This tension between fantasies of racial supremacy and realities of racial diversity remains one of the supreme challenges facing the United States, and thus our churches, today. When the Los Angeles riots seared the conscience of the nation almost twenty years ago, it was the *second* time I had seen my city burn. Both the 1965 and 1992 riots—the latter being the largest "domestic disturbance" in the United States since the Civil War—occurred because of the violence and dehumanization of persistent racism and social inequality and our refusal to have meaningful public conversation about it. History shows repeatedly that the "cold war" of frozen race and class relations inevitably erupts into the heat of built-up rage. As James Baldwin famously wrote in his 1963 *The Fire Next Time*, "We may be able, handful that we are, to end the racial nightmare, and achieve our country and change the history of the world. If we do not now dare everything, the fulfillment of that prophecy, recreated from the Bible in song by a slave, is upon us: 'God gave Noah the rainbow sign; no more water, the fire next time!'"

It is no overstatement, then, to say that the future of North American society—the same can be said of the human experiment as a whole—depends upon our ability to live peaceably and justly with human diversity. The question is whether we can, in church and in society, forge models of coexistence-with-congruence rather than unity-by-uniformity. Thus this opening biblical reflection begins our approach to the immigration debate by looking at two related texts, one from each Testament, which concern the key issues of cultural heterogeneity, social health, and human freedom.

Imperial Homogeneity: Babel

One of the key characteristics of human diversity is language. A recent study found that almost half of the 1.3 million students in public schools throughout Los Angeles County spoke a language other than English at home, with more than eighty languages represented. Soon, those who speak Spanish as a first language will be a majority in California. In reaction to these demographic realities, there is growing resistance to linguistic diversity throughout the United States, the most notorious being state laws declaring English as the "official language." English-only organizations have become increasingly vocal, often operating synergistically with anti-immigrant groups. They press for substantive restrictions, such as dismantling multilingual state services and bilingual educational programs. Employers are insisting that employees speak only English on the job, and cities are passing laws dictating what languages can appear on commercial signs. While this backlash comes from a variety of factors, one is ethnocentrism, about which scripture has something to say.

One of the earliest stories in the Bible is a warning tale about the correlation between ethnocentrism, empire, and human oppression—and it begins with the ominous phrase "Now the whole earth had one language" (Gn 11:1). The ancient fable of the Tower of Babel (11:1–9) represents the culmination of the primeval Creation narrative of Genesis 1–11. This text probably dates to after the collapse of the Israelite monarchy, written amidst the bitter experience of exile in Babylon. Knitting together ancient Semitic tales and Mesopotamian myths, and peering deep into their collective past, Israelite scribes composed a story of origins that represents a sober reassessment of their people's own experiment with urban civilization. The revolutionary argument of Genesis 1–11 is that the failure of the Jerusalem-based monarchy was not just a *national* disaster; it was a symptom of the much deeper *anthropological* problem of empire.

Genesis begins with a lavish description of the unqualified goodness of the original Creation, in which "the human Being" enjoys symbiotic communion with God and nature (1–2). However, the human delusion that perhaps things are not good *enough* intrudes (3:1–7), issuing in a series of archetypal violations that signal a steady deterioration of our condition, known in Christian theology as "the fall." Alienated labor (3:17–19) leads to fratricide (4:1–16), which leads to the ultimate human attempt to reengineer the world: the building of a city (4:17). In its wake come the logic of vengeance (4:23f), the rise of a warrior class (6:4), and a world "filled with violence" (6:11).

Despite a divine effort to "start over"—Noah's rescue project on behalf of all living things (6:13–9:29)—the fall narrative deepens after the Flood story. The first post-Diluvian genealogy is etiological, describing the origins of city states in Mesopotamian antiquity. Ham's sons represent a new, "predatory" line (10:6), which includes *Mizraim* (the ancient name for Egypt), *Canaan* (the infamous Egyptian vassal state that later in the biblical story becomes Israel's arch enemy) and *Cush* (associated with the Early Dynastic period around 2800 BCE; an ancient Sumerian king list names Kish as the place where civilization resumed after the Great Flood). Cush's most notorious son, in turn, is Nimrod, given the curious moniker "mighty hunter."

Nimrod's progeny reads like a litany of imperial kingdoms (10:8–10):

- *Babylon*, where the authors of Genesis were languishing in captivity;
- *Erech*, probably Uruk, in Sumerian lore the seat of the second dynasty after the flood, which included the famous Gilgamesh; and
- *Accad*, founded by the great Sargon (ca. 2300 BCE).

All of these are located on the "plain of Shinar," a biblical euphemism for the Fertile Crescent—and mythic site of the Tower of Babel. "From there Nimrod went on" (10:11) to seed empires in *Asshur* (Assyria), including Nineveh (featured in the prophetic books of Nahum and Jonah) and Calah "the great city" (rebuilt by Shalmaneser I in the mid-thirteenth century BCE, and today known as—*Nimrud!*).

These aggressive city-states were "mighty hunters" indeed. "Urban civilization is warring civilization," wrote Jacques Ellul in *The Meaning of the City* (1970); "conqueror and builder are no longer distinct." Indeed, the progressive fall narrative of Genesis 1–11 correlates broadly with what we know about the rise of agrarian civilization in the late Neolithic period. For millennia, human band societies universally followed sustainable hunter-gatherer life ways. But with the domestication of plants and animals beginning around 10,000 BCE, a slow but steady transformation in human habitation patterns commenced. The "agricultural revolution" led to increasingly sedentary lifestyles and growing food surpluses, which in turn led to population increases. Village social organization became steadily more complex and hierarchical, as emerging command economies came under the management of new military and political elites. Hunter-gatherers no more voluntarily embraced these new ways than did native peoples rush to join European colonizers after contact in the Americas. Rather, through loss of habitat and conquest, they were forced into peasant servitude by predatory farming societies with a voracious appetite for land and labor. Pointedly, the first murderer in the Genesis story is the farmer Cain, whose progeny builds the inaugural city (Gn 4).

This process happened independently in several parts of the world over several millennia, and the earliest archeological evidence to date of a walled city is probably Catal Huyuk in Turkey (ca. 6000 BCE). But it appears to have first triumphed in Mesopotamia (in the parlance of Genesis 3:24 and 4:16, "east of Eden"), where delta waterways were harnessed for irrigated farming and the emergence of the first imperial city-states. Not only did the Semitic tribes to the west have front-row seats for this unfolding, disastrous drama, they were also among its first victims. This suggests that the old traditions lying behind the Genesis narrative represent perhaps the world's first literature of resistance to civilization-as-empire.

An origins story that began in a garden now culminates in a tower. The ancient folktale about "Babel" in Genesis 11 best expresses the antipathy of those living in the oppressive shadow of the great city-states. It opens by reiterating the migration of people eastward (11:2a)—that is, further *away* from Eden. The "plain of Shinar" symbolizes Mesopotamia, and the building project there represents the centripetal power of urban empire. Life in Babel is fundamentally characterized by centralization of purpose (the construction of a tower) and cultural conformity (they all spoke one language). The metropolis exerts an overwhelming gravitational force (both economic pull and military push) to bring human and natural resources into its orbit, expropriating and concentrating economic and social assets. "Adam Smith said it once and for all," wrote William Appleman Williams in his classic book *Empire as a Way of Life* (1980). "The city enjoys and exploits a structural advantage over the country. . . . The essence of imperialism lies in the metropolitan domination of the weaker economy (and its political and social superstructure) to ensure the extraction of economic rewards."

The note in Genesis 11:3 that construction materials consisted of "bitumen and baked brick"—a standard for-

mula in Babylonian building inscriptions—sharpens the
polemical edge of the tale. It is a specific allusion to the
Hebrew's experience of slavery in Egypt, summarized so
succinctly in Exodus 1:

> The Egyptians set taskmasters over the Israelites to
> oppress them with forced labor. They built supply
> cities, Pithom and Rameses, for Pharaoh. . . . The
> Egyptians became ruthless in imposing tasks upon
> the Israelites, and made their lives bitter with hard
> service in mortar and brick and in every kind of field
> labor. (Ex 1:11, 14)

Those "storehouse cities" served two purposes: projecting
Egyptian military power into the province of Canaan and
serving as collection points for the extraction of tribute
from vassal cities and villages there. The human cost of their
construction was born by those at the bottom of the social
pyramid. The Hebrews had reason enough to resent the
towers their slave labor created.

Israel's prophets later routinely denounced the towers of
fortified cities, which symbolized the architecture of domination and the idolatrous hubris of empire. "Ponder the
former terror," wrote Isaiah; "where is the one who took
the tribute, the officer in charge of the towers? You will
see those arrogant people no more" (Is 33:18). For Zepha-
niah the "day of the Lord" brings "trumpet and battle cry
against the fortified cities and against the corner towers"
(Zep 1:16). And Gideon's vow to the men of Peniel articu-
lates an Israelite guerilla's defiance of imperial hegemony:
"When I return victorious, I will tear down this tower"
(Jgs 8:9). Prophetic judgment oracles often echo Genesis

11: "You said in your heart. . . . 'I will ascend to the tops of the clouds, I will make myself like the Most High'" (Is 14:13f). "Even if Babylon reaches the sky and fortifies her lofty stronghold, I will send destroyers against her, declares the Lord" (Jer 51:53).

Babel's tower is a thinly veiled reference to Babylon's grandiose ziggurats (an inscription from ancient Nippur describes a ziggurat "whose peak reaches the sky"). Evan Eisenberg, in his brilliant *The Ecology of Eden* (1998), argues that the ziggurat (or pyramid) represented an "artificial mountain" upon which the gods could conveniently be consulted by the king. Ancient peoples traditionally acknowledged mountain peaks as sacred—a cosmology Israel shared, as evidenced by the Exodus narratives of Moses' rendezvous with YHWH on Sinai (Ex 19, 24). This reverence, says Eisenberg, was "mythic shorthand for ecological fact," namely, a primal appreciation that water, weather, and wildness flow down from the mountains, resourcing and regulating all downstream ecosystems. But imperial urban societies sought to domesticate nature, bringing the wild sacred "into captivity." Atop the engineered mountain the king communed with deities who were also domesticated as patrons of the empire. The peak that traditional peoples looked *up at* reverently as the source of life and power was now replaced by a dominating tower from which the ruler and his gods looked *down on* their subjects in surveillance and control.

The pathology of all this is summarized in the satirical word play of Genesis 11:9:

"it was called *babel*" (the Akkadian *babil* meant "gate of the gods")
"because there the Lord confused (Heb. *balal*) them."

Israel's scribes believed that imperial tower builders were deeply confused about the proper human relationship to both the divine and the natural. The tower story thus unmasks these seductive civilizational heights as the *nadir* of the human fall from original communion. It was a brilliant polemical counterattack on the cosmology of empire.

These ancient sages understood well the deadly threat of concentrated human ingenuity in the service of an imperial state: "Now there is nothing they propose to do that will be impossible for them" (11:6). The terrible truth of that warning is only now dawning on us moderns, living as we do under the Damoclean swords of historical technological end-games: ABC (atomic, biological, and chemical weaponry), GRN (genetic, robotic, and nanotechnologies) and the ecological crisis of climate change resulting from human engineering. The uncanny correlation between massive state construction projects and imperial ambition is ubiquitous today, from Mulholland's aqueduct to the Manhattan Project to deep-sea oil drilling (I write on the anniversary of the Deepwater Horizon disaster in the Gulf of Mexico). This impulse is of course celebrated as the engine of our modern civilization; but according to Genesis, it expresses the ultimate logic of the fall, placing the whole human experiment at risk. Yet interestingly, the real focus of Genesis 11 is not so much the wrong-headed engineering project, but the problem of imperial *monoculture*.

The same divine "council" that created human beings in Genesis 1:26, only to have to expel them from the garden in 3:22, must now reconvene to deconstruct Babel: "Come, let us go down and confuse their language" (11:7). This is *not* intended as an etiological account of how people came to speak so many different languages. Rather, the overall scheme of Genesis 1–11 suggests that this concluding warning tale asserts that the way to resist the social and political forces of centralization is to reassert the Creator's original intention that human communities be "scattered abroad over the face of the earth" (1:28, 9:1). The divine antidote to the centripetal, homogenizing project of empire is a redispersion of peoples (11:8), symbolized here by both linguistic/cultural variety and geographic diffusion.

This "scattering" is portrayed in Genesis not as the tragic result of God's judgment, as is usually preached in our churches, but rather as an act of *centrifugal* liberation from urban monoculture and superconcentration. This archetypal movement from center to margins finds further articulation in two foundational stories in Torah. The first comes hard on the heels of the Babel account: Abram's call out of the metropolis of Ur to the peripheries of Canaan commences the great biblical narrative of redemption as counterpoint to the fall (11:31–12:5). The second is the Exodus story of emancipation from Egyptian captivity, in which the Hebrews are led into a wilderness experiment that seeks to rehabilitate the older, preimperial life ways of gift economics (Ex 16) and "retribalization" (Nm 1–3; on the first see Myers 2001; on the second, see Gottwald 2009 and Howard Brook 2010).

The ancient Israelites, having been repeatedly displaced or colonized by urban civilization, seem to have developed a paleo-psychic impulse toward such centrifugality. This is best summarized in the Psalmist's later reiteration of Babel's lesson:

> Truly, I would flee far off; I would lodge in the wilderness . . .

Confuse, O Lord, confound their speech, for I see violence and strife in the city.
Day and night they go around it on its walls, and
iniquity and trouble are within;
Ruin is in its midst; oppression and fraud do not depart from its marketplace. (Ps 55:7, 9–11)

Israel's survival was predicated upon resistance to succes-
sive empires through the stubborn maintenance of its own
cultural, linguistic, and religious distinctiveness and noncon-
formity (see Horsley 2008).

Centuries later, Jewish Christians surrounded by the dominating architecture and homogenizing social forces of the Roman Empire renewed this ancient tradition of resistance, as
narrated in Luke's story of the birth of the Christian church.

Insurrectionary Heterogeneity: Pentecost

Why is the "scattering" portrayed in the Babel tale
equated with diversification of language (Gn 11:7)? Perhaps it recognizes that language is one of the fundamental
things that makes us human and that linguistic distinctiveness characterized the original forms of human organization before the rise of imperial monocultures. The ancient
wisdom preserved in this story reminds us that cultural heterogeneity is as essential to human social ecology as species diversity is to a healthy biosystem. This very point was
made by the International Society of Ethnobiology's 1988
Declaration of Belém: "There is an inextricable link between cultural and biological diversity."

Today, more than half the world's population resides in
cities, as compared with about 9 percent a century ago. In

many ways, the entire globe is becoming a vast, networked metropolis. This is neither accidental nor the inevitable result of human "progress," but the result of five hundred years of European imperialism, which has systematically eroded local cultures and imposed the colonizer's language and culture on conquered peoples. The erosion of human diversity is accelerating today with the revolution in global communications, the opening of trade barriers and ascendancy of multinational corporations, and the mobility of populations (from leisure travelers to displaced refugees to immigrants). Ethnic costumes are giving way to Tommy Hilfiger, traditional chants to Madonna, and regional cuisine to McDonalds. Human variety, like species diversity, is falling victim to global capitalism. The new Tower of Babel is the banal conformity of commercial culture and transnational technocracy.

Terralingua (http://www.terralingua.org), founded in 1996 to defend biocultural diversity, warns that "global economic, political, and social forces are eroding the vitality and resilience of the world's ecosystems and cultures. A 'converging extinction crisis' is leading to a rapid and vast loss of diversity in all its forms." And if language is, as the old Bible story suggests, the barometer, then we are truly in trouble:

> More than 95% of the world's spoken languages have fewer than 1 million native speakers. Half of all the languages have fewer than 10,000 speakers. A quarter of the world's spoken languages and most of the sign languages have fewer than 1,000 users… It has been estimated that 20–50% of the world's languages are already moribund, and that 90% (possibly even more) may be moribund or will have disappeared by 2100.

The only solution is a new sort of "scattering." Terralingua advocates that every language, along with its variant forms, is inherently valuable and worthy of being preserved and perpetuated, regardless of its political, demographic, or linguistic status; that deciding which language to use, and for what purposes, is a basic human right inhering to members of the community of speakers now using the language or whose ancestors traditionally used it; and that such usage decisions should be freely made in an atmosphere of tolerance and reciprocal respect for cultural distinctiveness. Again, we find that scripture addresses this very struggle.

The story of Pentecost reenacts the divine antidote to Babel's imperial homogeneity by again reasserting human cultural diversity. Acts 2 narrates the inauguration of the church in the power of the Holy Spirit—though what *sort* of practices the Spirit empowered has been a divisive issue among Christians ever since. Today ecclesial debates about what it means to be "Spirit-filled" usually focus on individual charismatic gifts rather on the church as an alternative social model. But in Luke's narrative, the Spirit ignited a multilingual eruption at the heart of cosmopolitan Jerusalem and in the face of Roman social control, in the long tradition of Jewish centrifugal challenges to centripetal empire.

The setting of the story in time and space is significant. It begins with the phrase "when the day of Pentecost was being fulfilled" (Acts 2:1; Gk *sumplērousthai*). This verb can mean "filled to completion," in which case it alludes to the end of the fifty-day celebration of the "Feast of Weeks." Originally an agricultural festival, the liturgical calculations of Shavuot echoed the Jubilee ethos (compare the 7 X 7 weeks in both Lv 23:15 and 25:8–10). This suggests that the Jubilee vision of periodic redistributive justice was supposed to inform *every* harvest (see Myers 2001). The verb could also connote a consequential "fulfillment of destiny," as it does in Luke regarding Jesus' journey to Jerusalem and the Passion (Lk 9:51). Either way, it signals something momentous.

The "house" in which the disciples are gathered (Acts 2:2) is presumably the same place as the "upper room" of Acts 1:13. As coconspirators with a leader who had just been executed as a political dissident, Jesus' disciples were in hiding from the authorities. However, in Luke's story the "great wind" of the Spirit transforms fearful fugitives into "bold" public witnesses (Acts 2:2–4). What begins in a safe-house attic ends on the streets of Jerusalem, as these Galileans return to the very place where Jesus was tried and condemned just weeks before. In other words, the church was forged by a remarkable act of coming out of the closet (as gays and lesbians would say), of breaking silence (as feminists would say), and of speaking inconvenient truth to power (as nonviolent resisters would say). We might think today of Latin American Mothers of the Disappeared or Palestinian Women in Black, refusing to cower before regimes of terror as they hold public vigil on behalf of victims of political violence. This is how the church was birthed, and every time we muster the courage to bear the same kind of witness in the power of the Spirit, the church is born *again*!

Luke's story of the Spirit's descent on the disciples consists of three parts:

- 2:1–13   the experience of "tongues"
- 2:14–41 Peter's speech and the response of the crowd
- 2:42–47 the discipleship community of goods

The first and third are brackets, beginning with "tongues of fire *distributed* among the disciples" (2:3), and concluding with church members selling their possessions and "*distributing* them to whoever had need" (2:45; the only two appearances of the Greek verb *diamerizō* in Acts). Here we see the centrifugal "scattering" impulse: a redistribution of both cultural and economic power. We will focus here on the first, because the mysterious "tongues as of fire" (2:2) symbolize far more than an ecstatic spectacle of *glossolalia*.

In Luke's larger narrative, this scene correlates to the wilderness prophet John's allusion to baptism "with the Holy Spirit and with fire" (Lk 3:16; Acts 1:5). But Pentecost's tongues are immediately put to the *practical* use of cross-cultural communication. Perhaps alluding to the gathering of peoples on the plain of Shinar (Gn 11:2), Luke reports: "Now there were dwelling in Jerusalem devout Jews from every nation under heaven" (Acts 2:5; the list of nations in 2:9–11 suggests "all four directions"). But these pilgrims (or are they immigrants?) begin to hear about the "powerful works of God" *in their own tongue*, something apparently so extraordinary that it is repeated thrice (2:6, 8, 11). This is because there was already a perfectly serviceable *lingua franca* available: Greek was the official language of the eastern empire. But the Spirit reaches through this veil of cultural conformity and Roman regulation, reanimating all the small, local languages. Is this not a profound affirmation of ethnic distinctiveness and rootedness in defiance of imperial assimilation?

The crowd's bewilderment (2:12) has as much to do with *who* is talking as with what is being said. Cosmopolitan visitors of high standing are unaccountably being instructed by rural, uneducated, but suddenly polyglot Galileans (2:7).

The authorities' astonishment at the erudition of such "un-schooled, ordinary men" is repeated later in the story, there explained only by the fact that "they had been with Jesus" (4:13). Luke has also made it clear from the outset that women are part of this discipleship group (1:14), and Peter confirms that females are indeed publicly participating in this prophetic revival (2:17f). Boundaries of race, class, and gender are being transgressed by the power of the Spirit. This is not a portrait of polite, organizational rhetoric about multiculturalism, much less of corporate or state-sponsored "diversity training." It is an in-your-face popular linguistic *intifada* amidst Roman occupation, declaring liberation from the underside in downtown Jerusalem.

The suddenly articulate Peter begins his defense of this cultural mutiny with a line that almost suggests vaudeville: "These men are not drunk, as you suppose; it's only nine in the morning!" (2:15). He then goes on to cite the very so-ber prophet Joel (Jl 2:28–32a), whose phrase "pouring out the Spirit" is notable because in most prophetic writings this verb (Heb *shaphak*) is used in relation to God's wrath (e.g., Is 42:5; Jer 6:11; Lam 4:11; Ez 7:8; Hos 5:10; Zep 3:8), not blessing. The blessing is this linguistic insurrection, a re-covery of the antidote to Babel. Yet there is plenty of judg-ment imagery in Peter's street preaching; indeed, the rest of his speech (Acts 2:22–35) takes aim at the very authorities who have just put Jesus of Nazareth to death.

"Let all the house of Israel therefore know assuredly that God has made this Jesus whom you crucified both *Lord* and *Messiah*," shouts Peter (2:36). He could not have been more politically volatile. His people were, after all, firmly under the boot of Caesar's "lordship," and all "messianic" movements were brutally suppressed by both the Roman and collaborating Judean authorities. Peter is challenging his compatriots to transfer their allegiance from executioner to victim (2:38). This kind of talk will shortly land him in jail (Acts 4), just as it did John the Baptist (Lk 3:8ff) and of course Jesus himself. Peter has taken up the baton from his fallen comrades; as Salvadoran Archbishop Oscar Romero put it shortly before being murdered by the U.S.-funded military as he celebrated Mass, "I will rise in my people."

Unlike so much of our contemporary social criticism and protest, however, behind Peter's scathing indictment of the public order is an embodied social alternative of a Spirit-filled church (Acts 2:42–47). By the end of Acts 2, the cringing little group of political refugees has been transformed into a dynamic community, in which Genesis diversity and Shavuot economic redistribution are being "fulfilled." Bread is broken, the scriptures are studied, and possessions are transformed back into gifts that circulate around "to whoever had need." The doors are open, and folk are being drawn in from the actions on the streets. We might well ask, with the onlookers in the story, "What does this mean?" (2:12).

In this multilingual insurgency Luke is affirming the diverse cultural contexts in which the new Christian movement would soon take flesh as the gospel spread throughout the Mediterranean world. But the echoes of the ancient Babel tale are unmistakable: "And at this sound the multitude came together and were *confused* because each one heard the apostles speaking in their own language" (Acts 2:6; Gk *sungcheō* is the same root word used in the Septuagint text of Gn 11:7,9). This is not, as it is usually misconstrued, a *reversal* of the alleged "curse" of Babel. Rather, Pentecost *reiterates* that tale's polemic and the divinely sanctioned strategy to deconstruct pathological imperial homogeneity by reclaiming cultural diversity. The gift of tongues communicates across linguistic differences *without* suppressing or eradicating those differences. *That* is what distinguishes true gospel mission from cross-and-sword conquest in the service of empire that has characterized Christendom all too often. Unity through the Spirit does not mean monoculture, but the celebration of human variety (see Myers 1994, 310–36).

The Acts narrative of Pentecost is a challenge to the entire order of things, personal and political. The Holy Spirit transforms human life inwardly and outwardly. She emboldens a working stiff like Peter, who has known shame and disgrace, to speak the hard truth to his own people in order to bring about change (2:38ff). And she empowers the gathered church to dance across entrenched (and legally enforced) boundaries of gender, race, and class in order to animate a movement that embraces "every tribe and language and people and nation" (Rv 5:9). Whenever this Spirit is poured out, our traditions and institutions will be disrupted and disturbed, not to mention our proprietary definitions of who "belongs" and who doesn't.

The local cultures around the world that are carried by today's immigrant poor have been eroded by centuries of colonialism and are in danger of being extinguished by the onslaught of global capitalism's drive for commodified homogeneity. The church must reassert the Genesis wisdom of a "scattered" human family by nurturing diversity, and must reaffirm the Pentecostal vocation of native-language empowerment. For in the great narrative of the Bible, God's intervention is always subversive of the centralizing project of empire and always on the side of the excluded and outcast, the refugee and immigrant. The Spirit has busted out and busted up business as usual many times since Babel and Jerusalem, and she is waiting to do the same in our own time—if *our* tongues would but dare to loosen.

2

Journey to the Margins:
Delle McCormick

Matthew Colwell

*From there YHWH scattered them over the
face of the whole earth. (Gn 11:9b)*

In the Tower of Babel story, God disrupts that archetypal imperial building project and scatters humanity into the richness of linguistic and cultural diversity. That same Spirit is at work in the Pentecost story, dispersing the faithful out to celebrate God's work in a wide array of tongues. And if those occupying places of privilege in the dominant culture of North America listen to that Spirit, they will often find themselves sent "down and out." Delle McCormick is such a person.

Delle was drawn by the Spirit away from the metropolis of her New York City high-rise and into solidarity with immigrants and the poor of Central America. In Cuernavaca, Mexico, Delle encountered vibrant new worlds of diverse language groups and met inspiring communities of impoverished people living out alternatives to empire. As a result, Delle began proclaiming the gospel in a new tongue.

Scattered: From New York to Cuernavaca

In 1989, Delle traveled to Cuernavaca for the first time. She went with a group from her Philadelphia Presbyterian church because the pastor's description had intrigued her. He called the journey "reverse-mission" for vocational discernment and said it could be life transforming. It seemed the right time to venture outside the boundaries Delle knew. She was living in an Upper West Side apartment, married to a successful financial consultant with a teenage daughter in the finest private school. She worked as a professional actress in soap operas and television commercials. But her heart yearned for a deeper encounter with the world around her. Promoting products as an actress felt vacuous, even disingenuous. Her husband's struggle with alcohol was worsening, and the walls of her high-rise felt confining.

Delle's pastor challenged the delegation to not let the trip be a *vacation* in Christ, returning affected but unchanged; instead he invited them to allow their *vocation* in Christ to be shaped by what they would see and hear. With the rest of her church group, Delle arrived at the Center for Intercultural Dialogue and Development (CCIDD), a retreat center that hosts visitors from all over the world. Delegations visit squatter camps and learn about the economic conditions and social history of the region, in order to hear, see, and consider issues of global injustice (http://www.ccidd.org). Delle's group went to the home of a woman named Gloria, who invited the Americans to take a seat and then told them the story of her Salvadoran village of El Mozote.

In December 1981, El Mozote was thought to be a safe haven from the violence of El Salvador's Civil War. It was a community of mostly Protestant Christians that had eschewed ties with the guerillas. Then members of the Atlacatl battalion of the Salvadoran Army arrived at her village. Gloria told of how they went to each of the twenty houses in the village to demand that occupants come out. They forced men, women, and children to lie face down as they were searched and interrogated. The soldiers then ordered the villagers to lock themselves in their homes for the night. The next morning, the military collected everyone and took the men to the village church and the women and children to a nearby house. Army personnel interrogated and tortured the men, pulling their heads back by the hair until they screamed and then decapitating them with machetes. After that, the women and older girls, including Gloria's mother and sister, were taken to various areas of the village to be raped, some repeatedly. The women were then killed, some with machine guns, others with machetes or strangled with bare hands. Finally, the younger children were taken outside to be shot, impaled with bayonets, or hung by the neck from a tree. Gloria lost more than thirty members of her family in the massacre (see Danner 1994).

Gloria went on to share how the Salvadoran Army had received millions of dollars that year in U.S. military aid and how the Atlacatl Battalion received training from American military advisors. Delle wondered aloud how Gloria could possibly invite this group of Americans into her home when it was their taxes that had financed these atrocities. Gloria answered: "You have to tell the story in order to heal. And you have to believe there is a good ending."

Delle found herself heartbroken and enlivened at the same time. She could no longer hold in her mind a portrait of God who sheltered people from suffering. Instead, she saw God alive and at work in the struggles of people like Gloria, suffering under oppression and violence, yet speaking truth and working for the transformation of the world. Delle resolved to maintain contact with CCIDD, and with Gloria in particular.

Delle returned to her Manhattan apartment and a lifestyle that included stretch limousines and stays at the Ritz Carlton hotel. But the disparity between that world and the poverty but authenticity she had encountered in Mexico was too painful to sustain. She dove into the subject of Christian discipleship as it related to lifestyle, economics, and power, devouring books out of Washington DC's Church of the Savior. She joined her church in a study of Ched Myers' *Binding the Strong Man* (2008), a commentary on Mark's gospel with a powerful critique of the dominant culture in North America and biblical models of faith-based resistance to militarism and empire. She participated in political protest—and started looking for a new occupation.

Delle felt she needed simple, honest work that could give her the grounding to consider her life's calling, and she found it in a Philadelphia farmer's market selling produce. Though her mother had sent her to charm school twice in the hope that she could avoid such a working-class fate, Delle found her new job oddly empowering. Though it paid a mere $6 an hour, it reminded her of the economic power she *did* have: the ability to earn a modest living with her hands. The produce stand proved fertile space in which to reflect on vocation. She recognized clients of her husband as they approached her to purchase vegetables, but they would often fail to notice or acknowledge her in return. She began to understand what it could mean to feel invisible as a laborer.

Other significant changes were taking place in her life. Her struggling marriage was heading toward divorce, and her heart and mind were drawn to seminary studies. When her marriage ended, Delle sold all of her things and moved to Massachusetts to study at the Episcopal Divinity School. Meanwhile, she kept in touch with Gloria and CCIDD. Gloria was part of an artisan's cooperative, and she delighted in their cloth weavings and other hand-crafted goods. So as in the first year of seminary, Delle traveled to Cuernavaca regularly, bringing the cooperative her material and pattern ideas, and taking their products back with her. Selling the crafts in the United States gave her the chance to tell the stories of the artisans, many of whom, like Gloria, had come to Cuernavaca fleeing the violence in Central America.

Halfway through seminary, Delle felt the centrifugal pull of the Spirit calling her back to Cuernavaca. She received a grant to study Spanish there, but when the five weeks were up, she stayed. Cuernavaca felt like the right space for her to deepen her solidarity with "people made poor," a phrase she used to stress how poverty was the result of concrete social, economic, and political forces. Delle took a job at CCIDD working as a spiritual director and trip leader, supervising the kind of "reverse mission" visits that had so impacted her own life.

After a year and a half, Delle returned to the United States to finish her studies and took on a new discernment challenge. Through psychotherapy and some honest self-reflection, Delle realized she was a lesbian. However, her denomination, the Presbyterian Church (U.S.A.), would not ordain openly gay and lesbian persons to the ministry. As she neared the completion of her Master of Divinity degree, Delle felt she had to leave the Presbyterian Church and entered a time of painful uncertainty as to her vocation. As Delle was walking on the seminary campus one day, a woman stopped her. Though the two had never met, she told Delle: "I had a dream about you last night. You weren't in it, only your hands, and they were serving communion. It was the most beautiful communion celebration I had ever attended—and when I saw your hands today as you walked by, I knew it was you!" Delle started to cry. She shared that she had indeed felt called to the ministry but was questioning it now. The woman replied, "I think I'm supposed to tell you that you are going to be a priest."

That dream would prove prescient, as Delle went on to become a pastor in the United Church of Christ. And she found her hands playing a critical role in her practice of ministry, seeking training in Reiki and other healing arts. Animated by the biblical portrait of Christ as healer, Delle sensed her call was to be an ambassador and agent of healing in a world full of violence and brokenness. With her seminary studies complete, Delle returned to her work at CCIDD, now as an ordained clergy person.

As the years went by, she sensed burnout creeping in. It was again time for a change, and she devoted a weekend to solitude and fasting. As that weekend of discernment neared its end, no answer had come. Disappointed, Delle sat down to dinner. Then the phone rang. On the other line was a minister friend who told Delle that the position of United Church of Christ missionary in Chiapas was open and that she should apply. Delle had previously shared with this friend her dream of one day traveling to the mountains of Mexico and working with some radical nuns. Precisely that job was now being offered. The thought of heading into a low-intensity war zone terrified her, but given the timing of the call and the unique opportunity it afforded, she took the post, now even further from her former life in New York City.

Healing for a World of Pain

Delle worked in Chiapas as an agent of healing and pastoral care to people primarily of Mayan descent. The violence in the region had left immense brokenness and suffering in these indigenous communities (for background, see Weinberg 2000). Delle taught spiritual disciples—meditation, prayer, and the labyrinth—offering tools for soul care so people could stay engaged in activism. And she offered healing hands. Trained as a nurse, Delle had long valued body care. Now in Chiapas, she found this call increasingly linked to her passion for peace and justice, which she also felt was healing work. She began to believe that her life vocation was to bring healing to all relationships—with God, with neighbors, and with the earth.

In Chiapas, people were often brought to Delle who were broken in spirit, hoping this "gringa" could have an impact. One morning, an emaciated twenty-seven-year-old man came, a Zapatista who had been well regarded in the community for his astute political consciousness and commitment to self-education. But a few months back, he had begun acting strangely. He could no longer recognize his own father, had stopped eating, and had tried to kill himself. Delle brought him to some of the nuns she worked with, who were also adept at Reiki. They were given permission to take the man's pulse and examine him. In the process, a terrible event from this man's past came to the surface. In a conflict over a woman, he had drowned a friend of his in the river, and now he felt like the river had his soul. Delle told him, "The Mother God forgives you, and wants you to go home." The man broke down in tears. Later, men from the community brought him down to the river, and he was invited to ask the river for forgiveness. He did so and was able to walk out of the river on his own strength. He then began a new life. It was one of many times Delle saw God's healing power working in Chiapas.

She took part in communal acts of healing too. One such ritual was in Acteal, located in southern Chiapas. More than a thousand people gathered on December 22, 1998, including international visitors from all five continents, to remember what had taken place one year earlier. Mexican paramilitary forces had opened fire on a group of indigenous *Tzotzil* who were meeting for prayer in a chapel. When the shooting and hacking with machetes had ended, forty-five men, women, and children were dead, including five pregnant women. Fifty-eight children became orphans that day. The attacked group was called the *Organizacion de la Sociedad Civil Las Abejas* (*abejas* means "bees"). They had formed five years earlier in response to land conflict and political injustice in Acteal and were speaking out against the growing bloodshed and repression in Chiapas. A member explained how they chose their name: "The bee is a very small insect that is able to move a sleeping cow when it pricks. Our struggle is like a bee that pricks, this is our resistance, but it's non-violent" (Tavante 2003, 5; see also http://www.lasabejas.org).

Delle gathered with the surviving *Abejas* to remember those who had been murdered. Rope was laid out on the hillside in the shape of a cross, and Samuel Ruiz, the bishop of the local Catholic Diocese, led a celebration of the mass. Partway through it, Bishop Ruiz said, "Don't be afraid. We are now going to reenact the massacre." Some of the *Tzotzil* villagers came out with wooden guns and machetes and pretended to shoot and hack at people. Then forty-five men, women, and children dropped to the dirt within the rope cross, including women with babies on their backs. For ten heart-wrenching minutes, no one spoke; all that could be heard was wailing and sobbing. Then a woman and a man came down from above the hill, representing a nurse and a priest, and started lifting up the fallen. The names of those who had died were called out one by one. Following each name, those gathered shouted "*Presente!*" Bishop Ruiz explained that as they took communion that day, they would be taking in the body of Christ and of all the people who have been broken in the process of peace and justice work. "They are a part of us now," he said. Struck by the power of that ritual of healing and resurrection, Delle thought to herself: "This is my calling; it is about being with the broken bodies of people, like those massacred at Acteal, and letting them be a part of me."

In the wake of 9/11 and the subsequent U.S. invasions of Afghanistan and Iraq, Delle felt called to bring back to the United States the good news she had encountered in Chiapas. She knew many clergy in the United States were feeling depressed because they did not know how to be prophetic in their U.S. context. Her time in Chiapas had provided her with a powerful story about both the good that is going on and the hard truth about empire. So she returned to "Babel" to try to lead others into a deeper solidarity with marginalized peoples.

In 2003, she embarked on a twelve-state U.S. speaking tour. One of her stops was at a church in Tucson, Arizona, where a United Church of Christ pastor named Randy Mayer had arranged for Delle to preach and lead a workshop. During her stay, Randy introduced her to the staff at Borderlinks, a Tucson-based organization that hosts trips of immersion and education along the U.S.-Mexico border (http://www.borderlinks.org). He also took Delle on a trip to fill water tanks in a remote region of the desert placed by Humane Borders, in order to provide water for migrants journeying north from Mexico through the highly trafficked Tucson Corridor (http://humaneborders.org). In that lethal stretch of desert, temperatures could reach 120 degrees, and migrants passing through it would often die from dehydration and hyperthermia.

By a water station, Delle looked down and saw the imprint of a little hand. She realized a small child had been passing through this hostile area of the desert, and her heart broke. A part of her felt called right then to be with those undergoing such suffering in that region. Her time in Cuernavaca and Chiapas had taught her that her own sense of joy, hope, and meaning was tied to her willingness to encounter suffering. Yet she sensed it was not the right time to move to Tucson, for she had another call to answer first.

Soon after, Delle was called to be the pastor of a United Church of Christ congregation in Barrington, Rhode Island. Known as "the white church," this upper–middle-class congregation was a far cry from Chiapas. But its members were eager to connect with the world outside their doors; some had been active back in the civil rights movement. They were open to exploring how they were connected to realities in Chiapas and other impoverished communities around the globe. Delle saw it as a chance to share the good news and began inviting them to be "scattered," preaching about a God who disrupts imperial projects and leads hearts, minds, and bodies to the margins. She spoke of what it means to be blessed and converted by oppressed people, and even led a delegation from her church to visit Chiapas, inviting them to see firsthand the context that had so impacted her. It was a challenging ministry but one that helped Delle better understand the complexities of living in the United States while simultaneously yearning for global justice.

While booking a trip for her church to spend a week with Borderlinks, she noticed they were seeking an executive director. The tug on her spirit that she had felt back in Tucson resurfaced. She read the job description and thought it was a perfect fit. In 2005, the centrifugal power of the Spirit now sent her out again, this time to the Arizona desert. At a time when so many of the wild spaces of earth had been destroyed by the forces of civilization, she would find the evocative wilderness outside Tucson enlivening. On the margins of empire she would again find her spirit blessed.

"*Tenemos agua y comida!*" Delle yelled to the trees as she walked along desert stretches looking for migrants who might need food, water, or medical assistance. As executive director of Borderlinks, Delle went on "Samaritan Patrols" once a month. She found the walks good for her soul, the panoramic view of the mountains providing a vivid reminder of the power, presence, love and provision of God. On patrol she could sometimes glimpse Baboquivari Peak, a sacred place to the Tohono O'odham people who believe this site to be the birthplace of humanity and home of the Creator *I'itoli*. The walks also reminded her of the suffering so many migrants endured in their desperate efforts to head north. As she interacted with them, Delle not only saw their humanity firsthand, but glimpsed her own in new ways. She was moved by factors invisible to the dominant culture, like their bravery in seeking a better life, or the rich culture and history of the Tohono O'odham, who had dwelled in the desert long before European settlers arrived.

One day on patrol, she spotted three men seated by the side of the road. She stopped to ask them what was wrong. Two of the men said the third had been vomiting and they feared he was having a stroke. Delle checked his blood pressure, pulse, pupils, and respiration, which were fine. She then told him she was a practitioner of trauma recovery and asked if she could perform a couple of those techniques with him. He gave his permission, and as she examined him, it became clear to Delle that he was sick with sadness. When she shared this, he started to cry, saying he had crossed the border more than twenty times. He worked in the construction industry in Tucson, but his children were in Sinoloa. He went home to them whenever he was able, but each time he did so, he had to cross back over to the United States afterwards. During this journey the thunder storms and host of snakes he had encountered had broken him apart. "I just can't do it anymore. I want to go home."

Delle told his companions that he was safe but that they were going to call the Border Patrol so he could get home. Rather than flee, the companions said they would accompany him back. Delle sat with the three men as they sobbed, and it struck her that we are all sick from sadness. She thought of how Americans get low-cost clothes and food because the migrants who produce them work in sweatshops or are picking fruits and vegetables for poverty wages. We are all getting sick from the human sadness the whole system generates. In that moment she felt near to God's sorrow.

In Tucson, Delle was introduced to a one-room "altar" created by the artist Valerie James. The room displayed personal items discarded by migrants in the desert. Under the scorching heart, migrants will often drop items as dehydration and hyperthermia set in. Delle's spirit was touched by the abandoned photographs, Bibles, baby strollers, and jackets surrounding her. She realized that friends of hers from Chiapas could have been the very people who had discarded them, since one in ten migrants heading through the Tucson corridor come from that region. Delle returned to the museum often, imagining her friends losing their lives to the ravages of the Arizona desert. She found it a place to recenter herself and to remember her call to accompany those who suffer.

As a gesture of solidarity with such migrants, Delle participated with some 250 others in the annual "Migrant Trail: We Walk for Life," a six-day, seventy-five–mile hike through the Sonoran desert. It is an annual effort of North Americans to better understand firsthand the plight faced by migrants. The organizers acknowledge that the walk does not accurately simulate the experience migrants face crossing the desert, since those who participate are accompanied by support vehicles, food and water, and medical attention. But these walks for life help raise awareness about the crisis occurring in the desert along the U.S.-Mexico border, where since the 1990s more than five thousand deaths have occurred.

An active hiker, Delle was struck by how difficult the eight hours of walking each day could be under the intensity of the desert heat. At one point she stepped on a thorn, which not only pierced the sole of her tennis shoe, but penetrated her big toe. A doctor who accompanied the group soon had it bandaged. Were she a migrant, such an injury might have proven fatal. One evening, as the group was camping in tents, Delle walked a short distance outside the camp for a bathroom break. She soon found herself lost. As the panic set in, each cactus and brittlebush looked the same, as her eye scanned her surroundings for clues to where the camp might be. She eventually made her way back, but she wondered what it must be like for migrants to navigate desert terrain with no more than the sun and stars to guide them. After the group arrived at Kennedy Park in the United States to end the walk with a ritual foot washing, they learned that six migrants had died in that very desert corridor over the course of their solidarity walk.

Delle worked with Borderlinks from 2005 to 2010, helping delegations learn not only how the Arizona-Mexico border is littered with the lost dreams of migrants, but about the increasing militarization of the border and its human cost. In 2011, she accepted an appointment as interim minister at First Christian Church in Tucson. She works as a spiritual director and as a Pace e Bene Agent for Non-violent Change (http://paceebene.org/), and she remains active in local humanitarian organizations such as Samaritans and No More Deaths (http://www.nomoredeaths.org), which with Borderlinks advocate for humane border policies and just global economic practices.

Rev. Delle McCormick faithfully followed the Spirit's bidding from the heart of empire to the margins of Mexico and the Southwest borderlands. She learned the gospel in many tongues and has faithfully translated it in word and deed back among her people. Her discipleship journey is a powerful example for those from the dominant North American culture who would discover Jesus among the immigrant poor.

3

Our God Is Undocumented:
Sanctuary and Prophetic Hospitality

Ched Myers

*The stranger has not lodged in the street; I have
opened my doors to the sojourner. (Jb 31:32)*

In 1982, the small Christian community of which I
was part in Berkeley, CA, hosted a then-unknown Mayan
human rights activist named Rigoberta Menchu. She had
fled Guatemala the year before, having lost her parents and
brother to the violence of the military junta. I can still
see her making tortillas on a little *horno* in our backyard,
and hear her talking quietly but fiercely about the war my
country was fighting in hers. Rigoberta was laboring to
found the United Representation of the Guatemalan Opposition, four years before the publication of her influential
autobiography and ten years before she was awarded the
Nobel Peace Prize for her courageous advocacy for justice.[1]
Those few days with her were my introduction to the immigrant rights struggle, as our community helped get the
Sanctuary Movement started in the San Francisco Bay area.

The Sanctuary Movement of the 1980s shaped a whole
generation of faith-based activists. It sought to put a human face on Central America's overt and covert wars

by transporting refugees to safety and sheltering them in churches along the way. This movement stood in the nineteenth-century tradition of the Abolitionists' Underground Railroad that transported fugitive slaves to Canada, a precedent that was reanimated a century later by churches offering refuge to draft resisters during the Vietnam War. I was mentored by several Sanctuary leaders: Fr. Luis Olivares in Los Angeles and Jim Corbett in Tucson, who have since passed on into the cloud of witnesses; and Gloria Kinsler, now retired but volunteering faithfully with our cooperative. Some of the movement's leaders were indicted by the Reagan administration for their actions (see Chapter 8). But eventually their work and witness helped put an end to the region's wars, if not to the continuing oppression of immigrants.[2]

Today the war on poor countries is often more economic than military, but the casualties are the same. Families are pushed and pulled from their homes by the displacing forces of globalization, their rights and dignity sacrificed to our first-world demand for cheap food and services. To respond to this painful new/old landscape of immigrant suffering, a New Sanctuary Movement has arisen in the past few years, offering refuge to immigrant families being torn apart by U.S. Immigrant and Customs Enforcement regulations.[3] This renewed movement offers our churches another opportunity to practice what New Sanctuary leader Alexia Salvatierra (2011) calls "prophetic hospitality."

At its most basic, the contemporary immigration debate is about fundamental values of hospitality and sanctuary. These values have deep roots in the biblical story and rest upon important theological and ethical premises worth exploring here.

A Theology of Welcome:
"Behold I Stand at the Door Knocking"

The responsibility of hospitality is perhaps the oldest custom on the planet. It was (and continues to be) endemic among indigenous cultures across the globe, representing one of the basic components of their traditional cosmology of grace. Just as sustenance from nature is a gift to be shared and circulated, so too shelter—what is given will come back around (see Hyde 2007). Once peoples became more settled, the obligation to offer at least temporary hospitality to "sojourners" continued. This was certainly true in the often harsh world of Middle Eastern antiquity, given the risks of desert travel, on one hand, and the realities of human displacement due to the political and economic forces of ancient empires, on the other. As we will see below, stories of welcoming the stranger are ubiquitous in the Hebrew Bible.

The word for hospitality in the Greek New Testament is further illuminating. *Philoxenos* and *philoxenia* mean "love for the foreigner" and appear in exhortations throughout the epistles (Rom 12:13; Heb 13:2; 1 Tm 3:2; Ti 1:8; 1 Pt 4:9). Love in this case is a concrete practice in which hosts reserve space in their hearts and homelands for outsiders. Our English word, by the same token, comes from the Latin *hospitalis* (a room set aside for a guest), *hospes* (host, stranger, or foreigner), and even *hostis* (enemy)! In contrast to modern, urban notions of domestic hospitality, which usually concern only lodging for friends and family, the ancient tradition is more fundamentally related to those who are *unknown* to us (see Pohl 1999).

The religious idea of sanctuary is similarly ancient, found among many cultures, and most commonly associated with the sanctity of an altar.[4] It is also articulated in one of the oldest stories in the Bible: Cain's murder of Abel. This primal episode of violation provokes an extraordinary, counterintuitive divine response: to *protect* the murderer who "should" be punished (Gn 4:15). The "mark of Cain" served as a theological warning to those who would retaliate, thus constraining the lethal logic of endless retribution (see Myers and Enns 2009, 63ff).

This principle of sanctuary was codified in Torah through the establishment of "cities of refuge" for those guilty of manslaughter. Six were named, three on either side of the Jordan—close enough, in other words, for someone being pursued by vigilante justice to flee to (see Nm 35:13–15; Dt 19). These villages were to offer asylum while the offender was awaiting trial and hospitality as long as he had to live in exile. French philosopher and Talmudic scholar Emmanuel Levinas (1994), in a reflection on the biblical idea of sanctuary for man slaughterers, offers a compelling reminder germane to the question of "harboring" undocumented immigrants. If "the man-slaughterer is the one who is half-guilty, since he has killed, and half-innocent, since he did not mean to kill," Levinas argues, then we are *all* man-slaughterers, since "we all participate in structures of oppression" unwittingly. So U.S. citizens who offer sanctuary are only "half-innocent," since we are part of a system that routinely displaces people. Undocumented immigrants who receive sanctuary, on the other hand, are only "half-guilty," insofar as they were driven to cross the border without papers out of desperation due to economic or political forces not of their making.

If giving shelter to *perpetrators* is a first principle in the Bible, then how much more should we be hospitable to *vic-*

tims of violence and injustice! Three archetypally vulnerable groups are commonly named in almost formulaic fashion: widows, orphans, and *strangers*.[5] Because YHWH "watches over" them (Ps 146:9), they have intrinsic rights to sustenance (Dt 14:29, 24:19f, 26:12f) and to human rights (Dt 27:19; Ps 94:6). And the prophets measure the health of the nation by how widows, orphans, and strangers are treated (Jer 7:6; 22:3; Zec 7:10; Mal 3:5), a topic we'll explore more in the next section.

But there is another, theologically startling characteristic of scripture: from beginning to end, *God too* is portrayed entering our world in the guise of a stranger in need of hospitality. One of the first divine epiphanies is YHWH's mysterious appearance in the form of "three guests" (Gn 18:1–8). Abraham and Sarah offer them food, drink, and shelter, and their hospitality occasions the great promise of progeny that launches the salvation story of an entire people (18:9f). This encounter, we might add, takes place but in nature, underneath the "oaks of Mamre," outside the political realm of the "official" overlords of Canaan, a land in which the host couple are themselves "strangers" (21:34, 23:4).

We can go further: the God of the Bible is consistently portrayed as "stateless," and we can reasonably add *undocumented*. This is in stark contrast to the patron-gods of the empires that surrounded Israel, who lived comfortably in the temples of the king. In the Exodus tradition, the wilderness God doesn't even have a *name*, much less "papers": the moniker YHWH means "I will be whoever I will be" (Ex 3:14f). God's voice summons Moses into a conspiracy for freedom from a burning bush *outside* the borders of, and in opposition to, Pharaoh's political and economic system. Inspired and led by this God, the Hebrews flee Egypt "in haste" (12:33), and wander in the desert as a people with no legal status—as political refugees still must do.

Thereafter Israel bore an alternative covenant identity underwritten by this "feral" God. The people struggled to build a free society in which "there shall be one law for citizen and sojourner alike" (12:49). Of course Israel eventually wandered from the original vision by establishing a royal state (see 1 Sm 8). Even then, however, the prophets continued to draw their authority not from the throne, but from the Word of God received in the wilderness. The Creator's actions in the world are unauthorized by any state, and YHWH refuses to be domesticated under *any* regime (including the Israelite monarchy; see, e.g., Jer 7).

The Second Testament continues in this tradition. The gospel story begins with Jesus' family fleeing violence as political refugees, pushed around Palestine by the imperial forces of Caesar and Herod (Mt 1–2; Lk 1–2; see Chapter 9). The adult Jesus not only characterizes himself as homeless ("the Human One has nowhere to lay his head," Lk 9:58), but *stateless*. "My kingdom is not of this world," he says before the Roman procurator (Jn 18:36). The evangelists also portray Jesus as a constant recipient of hospitality who sometimes even "invites himself in" (see, e.g., Lk 19:5). Moreover, Jesus insists that his "dependent" status should be embraced by disciples, instructing us to conduct our missionary efforts not as a projection of power but as vulnerable itinerants reliant on the hospitality of those to whom we are sent (Mk 6:8–11). How different the history of Christianity would have been had *that* simple stipulation been heeded!

Executed as a dissident and buried like a common criminal, Jesus "suffered outside the gate" of the metropolis, and it is *there* that believers are told to encounter him (Heb 13:12f). Moreover, the early church believed that Jesus' resurrection did not resolve his marginalized social condition but *intensified* it. He appears unrecognized as a wayfaring stranger in the Emmaus Road story of Luke 24. And Matthew 25 portrays the risen Christ as hidden in the world among the marginalized: if we want to commune with *him*, we must show hospitality to *them*.

The Apostle Paul reflects theologically on this mystery in terms of *kenosis*, the "self-emptying" of Christ (Phil 2:5–8; see 2 Cor 8:9). He specifically links this theological assertion to the ethical practice of "each looking to the interests of the other" (Phil 2:4). As an itinerant missionary and worker himself, Paul understood how critical an "open door" was to his work (1 Cor 16:9; 2 Cor 2:12). "Contribute to the needs of the saints," he exhorted, "extend hospitality to strangers" (Rom 12:13). Indeed, Paul's ecclesiology is articulated as a revolving christological circle of hospitality: "Welcome one another, therefore, just as Christ has welcomed you" (Rom 15:7).

Luke's story in Acts of the church's early growth depicts the Spirit animating disciples to move boldly across borders of culture and nation, with or without "papers" (see Chapter 1). One of the riskiest episodes of hospitality involves the believer Ananias, underground in Damascus, who is ordered by the Spirit to welcome not a stranger but the notorious official in charge of jailing and executing Christians, Saul of Tarsus (Acts 9:10–19)! And when Saul becomes the "turncoat" Paul, fellow Christians conspire to smuggle him out "across the border" to escape the inevitable political backlash from the authorities he formerly served (9:23–25).

This episode brings to mind Bob Ekblad's compelling reading of the Pauline notion of God's grace that delivers us from the "Law" of death, in a trope proposing Jesus as "El Buen Coyote." Undocumented immigrants, he explains, are often smuggled over the border by "coyotes," and all have stories of both "bad" treatment along the journey (abuse, rape, abandonment, exploitation) and "good" treatment (honesty, provision, respect).

> Whether *coyotes* are good or bad, however, their work is illegal. This provides a strong contemporary metaphor to Jesus' role as Savior according to Paul's theology. Jesus can be viewed as comparable to a *coyote* in his embrace—his "crossing"—of people who cannot fulfill the legal requirements to enter legitimately into the reign of God. Jesus eats with tax collectors and sinners, heals on the Sabbath, touches lepers, and speaks with Samaritans—practices that mark him as an alien smuggler. The Pharisees, scribes, and other religious authorities in the gospels could be seen as analogous to the Border Patrol and other contemporary law-enforcement agents, who consider it their job to keep "illegal aliens" out. (2011, 164)

Ekblad concludes that "Jesus is such a good *coyote* that he actually gets caught by the Border Patrol agents of his time, while the real lawbreakers run free. His work undoes the legal basis for borders or barriers of any kind, destroying distinctions based on compliance with laws, and making everyone children of God" (165).

Finally, at the close of our scriptural canon, John the Revelator (himself a political prisoner in exile) portrays Christ approaching the church in the guise of a stranger seeking shelter: "Listen! I stand at the door, knocking; if you hear my voice and open the door, I will come in and eat with you" (Rev 3:20). This image of the "homeless Christ" comes at the culmination of John's seven letters to the churches. Interestingly, the last city addressed is Laodicea, a fortress that functioned as "guard and door-keeper" on the strategic road running from Ephesus to Syria (Ramsay 1905, 413f). For John, a central challenge to the churches of Asia Minor was whether they would dare to open their door to share a meal with Christ the stranger, until the day when the New Jerusalem dawned as a city whose gates never close (Rev 21:25). From Genesis to Revelation, then, hospitality is a *theological* issue.

An Ethic of Identity:
"A Wandering Aramean Was My Ancestor"

A second rationale in scripture for prophetic hospitality focuses not upon God's character but on that of the people. Israel was to act kindly and justly toward immigrants because they mirrored her *own* roots in the story of "a wandering Aramean" (Dt 26:5). One of the most repeated warnings in Torah cautions against mistreatment of resident aliens "because once you were yourselves sojourners and strangers" (see, e.g., Ex 22:21; Lv 19:33f; Dt 10:19). The book of James puts it rather more sharply: "If a brother or sister is in need and you say to them, 'Go in peace' and do not meet their needs, what is the good of that?" (Jas 2:15f).

There is an old story from the book of Judges about immigrants providing hospitality to immigrants. It concerns a Levite from the far away hill country of Ephraim who was traveling through Judah, returning home. As his party neared Jerusalem it was late, so his companions suggested that they spend the night there. But the Levite said, "We do not belong to this people; we will continue on" (Jgs 19:10f). They made it to the village of Gibeah (in the land of the tribe of Benjamin) as the sun went down.

> He went in and sat down in the open square of the city, but no one took them in to spend the night. At evening there was an old man coming from his work in the field. He was also from the hill country of Ephraim, but was residing in Gibeah. When the old man looked up and saw the wayfarer in the open square of the village, he said, "Where are you going and where do you come from?" The traveler answered, "We are passing from Bethlehem in Judah to the remote parts of the hill country of Ephraim, from which I come. . . . Nobody has offered to take me in . . ."
>
> The old man said, "Peace be upon you. I will care for all your wants; do not spend the night in the square." So he brought him into his house, and fed the donkeys; they washed their feet, and ate and drank. (Jgs 19:15–21)

There is, as we will see shortly below, a lot more to this story. But for the moment, the point I want to highlight is that while the *residents* of Gibeah ignored the travelers, leaving them outside in the plaza, it was the *immigrant* who offered hospitality. Remembering who we are matters.

Our middle-class churches in North America forget that the biblical writings were born not from privilege, affluence, and influence, but rather from struggle, poverty, and obscurity. But despite the Bible's warnings, we have lost sight of the fact that most of our ancestors, too, were immigrants—many of them undocumented! The tendency to obscure our origins with ethnocentric presumption goes back to the earliest days of European America. In 1751, for example, Benjamin Franklin—whose father was an English immigrant and whose mother came from Puritans who had fled from King Charles I—worried about German farmers settling in Pennsylvania. "Why should the Palatine Boors be suffered to swarm into our settlements and, by herding together, establish their language and manners to the exclusion of ours? Why should Pennsylvania, founded by the English, become a colony of aliens who will shortly be so numerous as to Germanize us instead of our Anglifying them?" (Delgado and Stefancic 1997, 258). Franklin also opposed increasing the African slave trade because he was concerned to keep the colonies "white in complexion."

Racist chauvinism and fear of the "other" have characterized every nativist movement since, so it should not surprise us that it lies under the surface of much contemporary anti-immigrant propaganda (see Chapter 8). It is precisely at the point we forget our roots that we become vulnerable to mean-spirited political currents that tolerate discrimination against, or promote criminalization of, undocumented immigrants.

Residents of the United States fall into one of only three categories:

1. The original inhabitants of this land, who have suffered a continuing legacy of displacement;
2. Those who were (and continue to be) *forced* to come here by economic and political forces such as slavery, war, or colonization; and

3. The rest of us, whose ancestors all migrated here under a variety of conditions—and in most cases, without proper documentation. (Mine came from Portugal, Mexico, England, and Austria.)

To ignore, fear, or scapegoat today's "sojourner," then, is to despise the deepest part of our *own* national story. Antipathy or even ambivalence toward immigrants and refugees indicates at best a profound suppression of our own past, at worst a deep, collective self-contempt.

Yet such attitudes are so common in the United States that one suspects there is something unresolved in our political unconscious. This may be attributable to the fact that for most people, permanent migration far from one's home to an unknown land only occurs under duress, and when driven by traumatic "push" factors, it can be dangerous, disorienting and stressful. This distress is then compounded by hostile reception and often systemic discrimination in the new place. It is, therefore, understandable that many immigrants would seek to move as quickly as possible past their liminal, pressured state as "newcomers."

There are two basic strategies for psychic survival under these circumstances: resistance and assimilation. In the former case, immigrants seek out and surround themselves with "Old Country" compatriots as much as possible, to minimize the pain and alienation (though such ghettoization is often externally enforced). Such communities maintain linguistic and cultural distinctiveness, and often aid other immigrants from "home." In the latter case, immigrants suppress their cultural-linguistic roots and differences, sacrificing ethnic "being" for a modicum of mainstream social "belonging."

In both cases, each subsequent generation tends to adapt more to dominant patterns. But this process moves more slowly in resistant communities, which tend to embrace identities as a cultural "hyphenates" (e.g., Greek-American or "1.5 generation" Korean-American). Of course, racial and class prejudices in the dominant culture often prevent full assimilation. Many minority groups are never fully accepted, regardless of their degree of cultural conformity (notably African Americans), and survive only through nurturing an *identity* of resistance. Assimilating communities, on the other hand, develop decreasing sensitivity to and tolerance of newer immigrants. At the point one's immigrant narrative has been effectively erased, as has happened with most Euro-Americans in the United States, there is no point of contact to constrain the development of beliefs that the "door should be closed" to those now perceived as too different, threatening, or burdensome.

Immigrant strategies of cultural resistance are not without social problems such as balkanization or permanent marginalization. But the process of total assimilation is more psychologically stunting and socially dangerous. As is the case with individuals, when groups deny a traumatized past, they must adopt "devised and dismembered" identities, such as myths of Manifest Destiny or white supremacy. These delusions fuel dysfunctional behaviors of repetition-compulsion, both personal (introjected violence) and political (projected violence). The suppressed immigrant past is then split off into a caricature of the immigrant "other" who is then demonized or dehumanized. Conversely, it has been demonstrated that survivors of trauma find healing only through the hard work of facing and psychically reintegrating experiences of distress or violation (for a longer discussion, see my reflection on "a nation of Esaus"; Myers 1994, 132ff).

Individual, family, and social health all depend on our willingness and ability to transact our past. It is thus a pastoral challenge to our churches to facilitate the process of "excavating" our buried immigrant identities, particularly in conjunction with discussions about contemporary issues of immigrant justice. Appendix 2 suggests some of the themes that might be explored in such work, and the Afterword reflects my own musings. Because the Bible continually reminds the people of God that "immigrants *are* who we *were,*" memory and solidarity are essential to our faith development. There will be congregational reluctance to this kind of engagement, of course, but this only serves to prove the point. But such reluctance is important to reckon with, and to that end it is worth returning in conclusion to our biblical story about hospitality in Gibeah.

The second part of Judges 19 grows *considerably* darker, as hospitality leads to hostility (Jgs 19:22ff). The village neighbors become furious at the old *campesino* for bringing home the foreigners he found in the plaza. Vigilantes attack his household, and end up torturing, raping, and killing the Levite's concubine. In a grim protest of the Gibeanites' shocking violation of the tradition of hospitality, the husband of the murdered woman cuts up her corpse into twelve pieces and sends one to each of the tribes of Israel. Outraged, the tribal confederation convenes a council (19:30), and agrees that this murder represents the worst crime since Israel came up from Egypt (20:4–7). A bloody civil war then ensues, with the Benjaminites ultimately defeated and Gibeah razed (20).

The awful rape and murder of the Levite's concubine became so notorious in later tradition that the prophet Hosea twice cites it as the archetypal crime of corruption (Hos 9:9, 10:9). The episode also apparently inspired the closely parallel (and more widely known) account of the angel travelers who were similarly attacked in Sodom, a violation that also ended in that city's destruction (Jgs 19:15–25— Gn 19:1–11). These are, of course, the same strangers hosted by Abraham and Sarah, as discussed above (18:1–8). That trope was rightly understood in the Second Testament as a *cautionary* tale: "Do not neglect to show hospitality to strangers, for by doing this some have entertained angels without knowing it" (Heb 13:2).

Judges 19–22 is one of the most difficult stories in the Hebrew Bible, centering around violent gender politics that are undeniably gruesome. I believe, however, that when read as a *parable* or even as a kind of *political cartoon*, the episode serves as a singularly urgent warning against the sin of *in*-hospitality.[6] To see this we must review its wider literary context. Judges offers various portraits of how the "Israelites did evil in the sight of Yahweh" (Jgs 6:1); the social vision of equality and mutual aid required by the tribal confederacy descends into corruption and selfish and predatory behavior. Judges is well known for its tall tales of war, idolatry, and deeply flawed heroes such as Gideon (7–8) and Samson (13–16). Our tale closes the argument of the book with a portrait of spiraling male violence, proving the point of the concluding refrain: "In those days everyone did as he saw fit" (21:25).

The groundwork for the travails of the Levite's concubine is laid in Judges 17, a story about a Levite "from Bethlehem in Judah" who travels to "the hill country of

Ephraim" looking for lodging and employment (17:7–8). A certain Micah, clearly identified in the narrative as an idolater (17:1–5), hires the Levite to serve his village shrine (17:9–13). However, a marauding group of Danite warriors soon also arrive, steal the Levite and the idols, and continue on to kill and dispossess the "peaceful and prosperous" people of Laish in order to set up their own idolatrous city there (18). On the heels of this tale and its implied denunciation of idolatry and aggression, we meet another Levite traveling in the reverse direction, from Ephraim to Bethlehem (19:1–3). This echo hints that we should read on with caution.

We are told that this Levite is pursuing an "unfaithful" concubine, and the lavish hospitality (which extends beyond the traditional three days) he receives suggests some sort of attempt at restorative justice by the concubine's father (19:4–9). Finally insisting on leaving to take his wife back home (19:10), the Levite begins the journey recounted above. Despite the inhospitality of both Jerusalem (!) and Gibeah (19:10b–15), the travelers are taken in by a fellow Ephraimite. It seems as if the happy circle of welcome and sustenance is completed: as he did at the concubine's home in Bethlehem (19:4–6), the Levite is washed and "eats, drinks and enjoys" (19:21–22a).

But what do we make of the patriarchal violence that follows? A plot that began with a *seemingly* minor sin of omission (leaving travelers in the square) here steadily escalates until the whole world is swallowed up in death. The local villagers show their hostility by threatening homosexual rape of the Levite, representing the ultimate act of humiliation in ancient Mediterranean male honor/shame culture (19:22). Desperate to protect the patriarchal honor of his guest, the one who offered hospitality now betrays it by offering instead to sacrifice his daughter and the Levite's concubine (19:24, echoing the refrain of indictment throughout Judges, "do what is right in your own eyes"). The supposed protagonist in the story, the Levite, follows suit by pushing his wife out the door (19:25, a complicit act that he neglects to mention in his subsequent demand for justice). The woman is ravaged, murdered, and then cut up by her husband (19:26–29). In reaction, a wholesale war against the perpetrators ensues, leaving tens of thousands of Israelites dead (20) and eventually more women killed and forcibly displaced as well (21).

To understand this misogynistic tale as a parabolic "negative object lesson" about the sanctity of hospitality, we must focus upon the threshold of the house as the narrative center of gravity:

- "no one has taken me into their house" (v. 18);
- "he took him into his house" (v. 21);
- wicked men surround the house, "pound on the door (Heb *delet*), and demand that the guest be brought out" (v. 22);
- owner "goes outside" to argue (v. 23);
- the Levite "took his concubine and sent her outside" (v. 25);
- the abused woman returns and collapses "at the door (Heb *petach*) and lay there until daylight" (v. 26);
- the Levite "opened the doors (Heb *daletot*) of the house and stepped out . . . there lay his concubine, fallen in the doorway (Heb *pethach*) of the house, *with her hands on the threshold*" (Heb *caph*, v. 27).[7]

This last phrase is too poignant to ignore: the woman expires clinging to the threshold of the house that was supposed to protect her in a village that was supposed to welcome her. The struggle over hospitality between those inside and outside the house culminates in a corpse at the doorstep, which signals more death to come as the sin of inhospitality unravels into all-out slaughter.

The Levite's act of dismembering the woman's *body* (an allusion to Genisis 22:10?), sending a piece to each of the twelve tribes, surely symbolizes how the *body politic* of Israel will be dismembered by the civil war between the tribe of Benjamin and the rest of the confederacy (see 20:23). The gender aspect to the story is also key: the female guest is the central victim here, *abandoned* by men rather than *protected* from them. If hospitality was a core value of Israel, women were essential to its practice. The concubine's destruction thus also encodes the fate of a people who put male (and tribal?) honor—and the violence that polices it—before the sacred trust of hospitality. What, then, is the cost of not welcoming the stranger? Nothing less than national disaster!

Such a parable may come as a disturbing surprise to comfortable and insular North American Christians. But it underlines how important the practice of hospitality is to biblical faith and warns against the spiral of violence resulting from its neglect. Perhaps only such a terrible lesson can wean us from our hard-hearted contemporary trends toward scapegoating undocumented immigrants and militarizing our borders.

The New Sanctuary Movement invites us to recover this core tradition of prophetic hospitality by experimenting with "harboring" undocumented people caught in an unjust immigration system. The story from Judges reminds us that such practices will inevitably run against the grain of both popular sentiment and government policy, as was the case in the Sanctuary Movement of the 1980s. But the theological and ethical traditions of scripture—even its grim "negative object lessons"—challenge us to recover our immigrant identities and to ignite our moral imaginations in the struggle for justice.

The undocumented God of the Bible and the refugee Christ stand forever at our doors knocking—at the *threshold* of our consciousness, our homes, and our national borders—waiting for us to remember the roots of our faith and identity, and to embrace a discipleship of prophetic hospitality.

4

From Immigrant to
Immigrant Justice Organizer:
Moises Escalante

Matthew Colwell

*The immigrant who resides with you shall be to you as the
citizen among you; you shall love the immigrant as yourself,
for you were immigrants in the land of Egypt. (Lv 19:34)*

Torah's call to the people of Israel to practice prophetic
hospitality because of their own history as sojourners serves
as a mantra for both the Interfaith Coalition for Immigrant
Rights and the New Sanctuary Movement. Moises Escalante
has served both organizations for years as an organizer, and
his own identity as an immigrant has shaped and supported
his life's passion to love other immigrants as himself and to
advocate on their behalf.

Fleeing and Facing the War in El Salvador

On Christmas Eve 1973, Moises, twenty years old, sat
in a Tijuana motel room with his younger brother Carlos
and a half-finished bottle of tequila. Carlos was not much
of a conversation partner, as a recent operation had left
bandages covering his jaw. Four days earlier, the two broth-

ers had taken a plane flight from San Salvador to Tijuana, where they were now waiting for a "coyote" to pick them up and take them across the border to the United States. Coyotes often take advantage of vulnerable migrants, accepting money and then failing to deliver the promised passage north. After four days of waiting and no word, Moises and Carlos were running out of money and options. Moises took another sip of Tequila and reminded himself that this coyote was the same fellow who had helped their mother successfully cross the U.S.-Mexico border four years earlier.

Her crossing took place in 1969—back when the economy of El Salvador had collapsed following the breakdown of a Central American trade agreement. Amidst the economic turmoil, his mother's combination restaurant/convenience store had gone under. Their father, a contractor, had also left the family in the wake of a bitter divorce, leaving their mother solely responsible for sixteen-year-old Moises, his fourteen-year-old sister Alejandra, and his eleven-year-old brother Carlos. With the loss of her business and break-up of her marriage, his mother asked herself the question that leads so many people to immigrate: do I remain where I am and watch my children starve, or do I seek work in another country? Her answer was to make the difficult journey north, leaving her children in El Salvador, hoping to send money to them soon.

Once in Los Angeles, she found work as a housecleaner and moved into a tiny apartment. She began to send money to her family at regular intervals, though to Moises, who administered the funds, it never seemed like enough. With his parents both out of the house, Moises had been left to care for his younger siblings. This was especially challenging given his brother's medical condition. Years earlier, Carlos had noticed a lump on his jaw, and further investigation showed it to be cancer of the bone. Now Moises was left to make the crucial decisions regarding Carlos's medical care, including whether to have surgery. He was careful not to pass on to his mother too many details of his brother's condition, fearing she might come back, thus depriving the family of their primary source of income. There were times that the money would get so tight that Moises would pawn household items like the television and radio.

Moises' education had been put on hold as well. In 1972, while studying sociology at the National University in San Salvador, he was on campus one day when he heard yelling during a class break: "The soldiers are here! They're beating up everyone!" Moises and the other students quickly fled campus and later learned that the National Guard had arrested teachers and students alike and carted away much of the university's equipment. Many of those arrested were never heard from again, and the university would remain closed for the next two years.

Starting to buckle under the pressure of managing a household, the teenage Moises joined friends who spent evenings out drinking. Yet soon after he woke up and knew something had to change. Moises had long resisted the idea of heading north, wishing to remain in the community where he had grown up. He had also been caught up in the anti-American sentiment at the National University, and was not eager to move to the United States. But with no other options in sight, he called his mother. "I'm ready to come live with you." His younger sister Alejandra had already moved to the United States three months prior, and it was time for him and Carlos to follow suit. Delighted to hear the news, his mother wasted no time in making the arrangements. She provided the money they would need to make it to Tijuana, where the coyote would pick them up for the journey across.

Moises and Carlos were now only a few hours' drive from their mother in Los Angeles but still stuck in a Tijuana motel. "Merry Christmas," Moises said to himself, and polished off the last of the Tequila. A week later, the coyote arrived. He brought Moises and Carlos to the road leading from Tijuana to "Las Playas," found a hole that had been made in the border fence, and slipped through. They ran for five minutes or so, and then hid, awaiting the arrival of a big green Cadillac they were told would soon arrive to drive them to Los Angeles. At 3 a.m. on December 31, the two boys were dropped off at their mother's little apartment.

Reunited for the first time in four years, it was awkward. Their mother was both familiar and somewhat of a stranger to them. Moises was taken aback by how small his new living quarters looked, especially in comparison to the big roads and lights he had just seen along the I-5 freeway. And he was already missing his neighborhood; at the stroke of midnight, Moises could only think about how he had celebrated previous New Year's Eves with family and friends back home. He felt isolated and out of place in the little Los Angeles apartment and privately began making plans to return to El Salvador.

With his mother working full time, Moises had few resources to draw upon. There were no community-based organizations to help, nor access to the Spanish-speaking television and radio stations that are prevalent today. He didn't know, for example, that he was required by law to register for the selective service or about the educational options available to a twenty-year-old. What he *did* know is that he needed to find a job. His first employment was helping his uncle on the grave-yard shift at a Westwood movie theater, cleaning from 9 p.m. to 4 a.m. Moises soon switched to running a taco and hamburger stand for $2 an hour—the federal minimum wage at the time. But this meant he could help his mother financially and begin saving for a car. He took on other work as well, holding down as many as three jobs at once.

By 1975, Moises was dating a young woman from Mexico, and as that relationship grew, his letters to a girlfriend back home trailed off. His dreams of returning to El Salvador in the near future also began to evaporate. He purchased his first car, and with his new Chevy and a good word from his girlfriend, Moises got a job as a driver for the typesetting company where she worked. In applying for the position he never needed to show a green card, proof of citizenship, or even his General Education Degree—a situation that has changed dramatically for immigrants today.

Moises was intrigued by the typesetting process and asked other workers how the equipment operated. The boss took notice of his interest and recommended that he take classes at the Los Angeles Trade Technical College (LATTC). He told Moises he was welcome to watch and learn inside the shop, so long as it was after hours. While some of the workers made fun of his English, others were generous with their time, showing him how to work the various machines. With their help and classes in typesetting theory at LATTC, Moises was able to work his way up from delivery person to assistant typesetter. He remained at that shop for fifteen years, eventually earning more than he would later as a human rights activist!

In 1979, Moises made his first return visit to his home country. He had gotten married in 1977 to a woman with

Legal Permanent Resident (LPR) status in the United States, which opened the door for Moises to become an LPR himself. Figuring he was in the United States to stay, the trip to El Salvador was to finish the application process and receive a green card. He hoped to visit relatives and friends, and figured he would get some overdue dental work done as well. The day he was at the dentist, there was yelling, chanting, and screaming outside the window. Moises got up from the chair to have a look. "What's going on?" Moises asked. "The new government is here," the dentist replied, "and things are changing in El Salvador."

As part of his visa process, Moises had a physical examination by a doctor who was a colonel in the Salvadoran military. Over the course of the exam, the doctor told him: "It's a good thing you are in the United States now. A lot of killing is happening here, and big things will take place in El Salvador very soon." Later, at his father's house, Moises learned that there had been a number of deaths in that very neighborhood. He was told about the killing in March of 1977 of Rutilio Grande, a Jesuit priest who was an advocate of liberation theology.

Moises returned to the United States wondering what all these developments would mean. For the past six years, his life had been consumed by his work and family life in the United States; now he took increasing interest in events taking place in El Salvador. His concern rose dramatically the following year when Salvadoran Archbishop Oscar Romero was murdered by government troops while celebrating mass. In 1982, Moises met some Salvadorans working in the United States to promote the peace process back home. In the wake of growing repression by the government and military, people were fleeing El Salvador in record numbers, and many of these new arrivals were anxious to do whatever they could to stop the killing back home. Moises took in a temporary houseguest who had once lived in his Salvadoran neighborhood. This man had participated in the peace movement and protested against the Salvadoran military, and had fled after a military offensive. During his stay, he would wake up in the night screaming, haunted by what he had seen. He gave Moises books and articles to read that examined the economic, political, and social situation of El Salvador.

The U.S. media was also drawing attention to El Salvador, with *Time* and *Newsweek* featuring stories on the violence and government repression. Animated by what he was learning, Moises started organizing meetings with others to strategize how they might show solidarity. He joined a growing movement called Casa El Salvador, which had connections to the Farabundo Marti National Liberation Front (FMLN); many of those involved had been driven into exile in the United States by the violence. Moises worked with El Rescate, formed in 1981 to provide legal aid and social services to Salvadoran immigrants, and Clinica Romero, begun in 1983 to offer mental and physical health services for Salvadoran war refugees. Moises hosted movies on the Salvadoran crisis which drew as many seven thousand attendees.

Moises was still working full time at the typesetting shop. Recognizing that this job provided him financial resources that many others in the peace and solidarity movement did not have, he kept working and contributing, though his volunteer activities now often required him to travel cross country. But as his political engagement grew, his religious life began to atrophy. Moises felt the church focused too much on the personal spiritual life and the heavenly hereafter, while his own heart was drawn to efforts that addressed concrete social and political realities here on earth. But this changed in 1985, when a Catholic priest, knowing of Moises' political bent, recommended he attend a workshop led by Jose Marin, a former missionary to Brazil who had spoken throughout the Americas on the Christian Base Communities Movement.

Reintegrating Faith and Politics

Moises was at a low point in his life, separated from his wife and headed toward divorce. He was demoralized in his political work, feeling that progress in the solidarity movement was elusive, and his own energies had sapped. And as an immigrant separated from his community in El Salvador, Moises found he was losing his identity. Who was he? What was his purpose in life? Moises attended the workshop with such questions close to his heart, hoping something he heard might fill the hole he felt in his spirit.

At one point in the workshop, Jose gave participants the following instructions:

Take your Bibles and notebooks with you, and go find a place by yourself for 30 minutes. Then open the Bible. It doesn't matter where you open it to, just open it and start reading. And think about what you read and what it might mean. Then think about the reality you see around you. Finally, think about how what you read in the Bible connects to that reality. Write down your thoughts in the notebook, and you'll have the opportunity to share with the group if you want to.

It was the first time Moises had opened his Bible in years, and his eyes fell on Ephesians 5:14: "Sleeper, awake! Rise from the dead, and Christ will shine on you." Moises was struck with a realization that Christ desires an *active* church not a passive one. "Our Lord wants a church that is engaged in the world politically, not that merely acquiesces to the status quo," he thought. "It's right there in the Bible!" The words on the page seemed to come alive to him, and he recognized how much he missed a vibrant religious dimension to his life. Jose Marin's articulation of a religious faith deeply connected to political liberation was galvanizing and enlivening to Moises at a time of deep spiritual hunger and of activist burnout.

Moises recalled with nostalgia the comfort and sense of direction his faith had once provided him. His mother had been a devout Catholic and raised him in the church. At age twelve Moises was already traveling to nearby villages to speak to public school classes about the value of prayer, the rosary, and the Catholic religion. He had even contemplated becoming a priest, and at fifteen, he had attended the Franciscan seminary in San Salvador. But the rigidity of seminary life, coupled with the separation he felt from family and friends, led him to leave after only a year. But he stayed involved in the Catholic church until the 1980s, when his growing political consciousness led him to downplay religious practice.

In this workshop, he was for the first time invited to connect *faith* and *politics, Word,* and *world*. His Catholic upbringing had never pushed him to consider faith's relationships to social justice or to "real world" issues like repression in El Salvador. As this workshop made this connection clear, it poured a new sense of meaning and purpose into his organizing and gave him new hope for personal and political change. He shared his reflections with workshop participants, then listened as others shared how scripture spoke to what was going on in the world around them. Fr. Marin then talked about Christian Base Communities that were cropping up around the world in impoverished and marginalized communities. Laypeople were reading the Bible and connecting it to their own context, discovering how it spoke to such issues as liberation from oppression, the importance of resisting violence, and how to stand against injustice (on this, see Cardenal 2010). As he listened, Moises heard a new calling; it now seemed to him that with God anything was possible.

The next year, Moises joined a group called Committee in Solidarity with the Church of El Salvador, supported by Fernando and Teresa Santillana, a Methodist couple from Peru heavily influenced by liberation theology. They helped Moises and others on the committee create a base community called Proyecto Adelante, designed as an outreach to Salvadorans who did not attend church because their faith and political activity was not sufficiently motivated by the message they heard there.

That same year, Moises was approached by Fr. Rogelio Poncel, a former Belgian priest who had previously worked in El Salvador to support Christian Base Communities. He invited Moises to an event called Living in Exile, intended to unite Salvadorans who had left the country with those still living there. The hope was that this connection might allow for strategic planning to bring an end to the civil war. This time Moises returned to El Salvador not as a tourist but as an underground organizer. He attended clandestine meetings with priests, nuns, and other religious workers behind closed doors, and discussed how the church could help end the civil war in that country, knowing that at any moment soldiers could barge in and take everyone away. Their analysis of the situation was that the FMLN was not going to defeat the government militarily, so it seemed that the best way to end the war and government repression was with a faith-based, nonviolent movement for peace (see Peterson 1996).

Moises returned to the United States feeling part of a wider movement, and he traveled to New York and Chicago, building connections and overseeing the creation of the Monsignor Romero Foundation, an institution designed to channel financial assistance to El Salvador. Moises also joined the Sanctuary Movement (see Chapter 8), connecting his advocacy for Salvadoran liberation with his Christian faith. He hoped this effort to provide shelter and protection to undocumented refugees would shed light on what was taking place in Central America, and could show U.S. citizens how their tax dollars were supporting repressive governments.

In 1988, Moises was asked to come to the Salvadoran village of Morazan to observe the pastoral work taking place in that impoverished war zone. When he first received the invitation, he thought this was crazy. "You want me to go to a place where guerillas control the area and are under attack?" As he thought it over, he recalled the words from Ephesians that God wants the church to "awaken!" Reluctantly, he agreed to travel to Morazan for a ten-day trip. Getting there was no easy feat. After flying into San Salvador, he was put on a bus and told to wait until a person came up to him and asked, "How's your house?" That person would be his next contact.

Along the bus route there were frequent checkpoints, and when asked where he was going and why, Moises replied that he was visiting his godfather in San Antonio El Mosco, a town (unlike Morazan) free of guerilla associations. At the end of the three-hour bus ride they walked for five hours. After enduring a downpour and further checkpoints, they arrived at a small village close to midnight, soaked and exhausted. At 5 a.m. he awoke to shouts of "the soldiers are coming" and quickly got on the road toward the next village. Three days later, Moises finally entered Morazan, with the pastoral team eager to meet with him. One member of that team was Rogelio Poncel, another Fr. Miguel Ventura, a Salvadoran priest who had been tortured for his ministry in communities like this one. Moises listened as they shared with him their struggle to live and support each other while under attack by the military. "It is our faith that keeps us going," they said.

At 2 a.m. that first night, Moises awoke to the sound of rockets in the distance. He had been sleeping fitfully on the floor of a small church where, he had learned upon arrival, a helicopter had recently dropped a bomb, destroying its main door. With that in mind, it had been difficult for Moises to sleep. He stepped outside to see where the blasts might be coming from, and off in the distance he saw three helicopters firing away. After watching for a short while, he went back to sleep, awakening again two hours later. He stepped outside to see small dots of light punctuating the darkness. He thought at first it must be a swarm of fireflies, but as his eyes adjusted, he realized they were the tips of cigarettes; members of the popular guerilla army were gathered and making plans for the day. He learned that a few of them had been a part of the shooting exchange with the helicopters earlier.

Moises felt like he had entered a different world. Back in Los Angeles, eggs could be purchased at a local store. Here in this little village, there was only one hen, and when it laid an egg, it was given to a member of the community who was sick or in special need. In contrast to the sense of isolation he had often felt in Los Angeles, here he had a powerful experience of community. For example, in the woman's coffee cooperative, decisions were made together as equal partners in a common venture. They talked about the Bible easily and often during their gatherings, noting how it connected with their reality and struggle. Moises was swept up in their ethic of sharing, freely donating his only extra pair of underwear to a woman who had just given birth.

A young village boy showed Moises a piece of shrapnel with the words "made in the U.S.A." printed on it. As he talked with those who had lost sons and daughters, the impact of the civil war weighed even heavier on his heart. He left Morazan with a renewed commitment to the churches in El Salvador and to bringing an end to the war. Back in the United States, however, the typesetting industry was undergoing significant change, with computers decreasing the need for the kind of skills he possessed. In 1990, Moises was laid off from his fifteen-year job, and needed to seek a new career. Shortly afterward, he ran into Don Smith, a Presbyterian minister he'd worked with on both the Interfaith Task Force on Central America and in the Sanctuary Movement. Don encouraged Moises to apply for a job at another justice-oriented nonprofit organization: the Coalition for Humane Immigrant Rights of Los Angeles (CHIRLA). His solidarity work and his own experience made him keenly aware of the struggles immigrants face, and CHIRLA was looking for somebody bilingual, bicultural, and familiar with the Los Angeles community. It was a perfect fit.

Moises spent a year with CHIRLA doing employment education until funding ran out a year later. He took the opportunity to return to El Salvador to take part in the peace process there. He helped organize forums and exposures around the country during the crucial last months leading up to the historic Salvadoran peace agreements of January 1992. Having supported the peace and justice movement there for so many years, Moises was deeply moved and considered remaining in El Salvador permanently. But a letter he received from his fourteen-year-old daughter reminded him of his responsibilities back in the United States. He returned home after five months and resumed organizing with CHIRLA, with whom he stayed for the next eleven years, educating immigrants on their legal rights, and the broader community about the contributions of immigrants.

His work included starting a rights program for day laborers, supporting them when they encountered police harassment, and education and advocacy around several California statewide ballot measures that affected immigrants. He worked unsuccessfully against Proposition 187 in 1994 (which would deny schooling, health care, and other benefits to undocumented immigrants); Proposition 209 in 1996 (which sought to dismantle affirmative action programs); and Proposition 227 in 1998 (which endeavored to dismantle bilingual education). These were difficult years for immigrant rights activists, but such defeats reminded Moises and CHIRLA of the importance of the work they were doing to combat the growing tide of anti-immigrant sentiment.

In October 1993, Moises was invited to go to Sacramento, the state capital, for the first time. The trip brought immigrants from Los Angeles north by bus to advocate for immigrant rights and educate participants about the political process. On this trip he met Ed Dunn, a Franciscan friar with a passion for supporting and defending immigrants. Ed's ancestors had emigrated to the United States from Ireland during the nineteenth-century potato famine, and after a perilous boat journey their port of entry—as it was for so many immigrants at the time—was Ellis Island. With all the crowds and commotion there, a seven-year-old member of the Dunn family got lost in the chaos, and they never saw or heard from the boy again. His disappearance was remembered by subsequent generations, including Ed's, which fired his commitment to see immigrants get to the United States safely.

In 1994, the same year Proposition 187 passed in California, Ed, Moises, and others formed the Interfaith Coalition for Immigrant Rights (ICIR), headquartered in San Francisco. As ICIR grew, they opened a Los Angeles office to enhance their statewide efforts, and Moises became its first director. His work involved educating immigrants on their rights and responsibilities, and trying to dispel myths in the broader community about immigration. He talked to the media, to elected officials, and to church groups about the facts concerning immigration, about just policies, and about how faith relates to the cause of immigrant dignity. He also emphasized how U.S. foreign policy impacts migration patterns, such as how the North American Free Trade Agreement intensified economic desperation in Mexico and Central America. And he focused on the history of immigration to the United States, especially how each time immigrants were recruited due to labor shortages, there was a reaction of nativism and anti-immigrant sentiment. He explained how the legal/illegal distinction prevalent today was not operative in prior waves of immigration, making it a less helpful distinction from a historical perspective.

Moises gave a high priority in his education work to scripture. On bus trips to Sacramento for political work, he would do Bible study with them on the way. Because fear is a primary concern for immigrants, especially as they consider political engagement, participants would open their Bibles to Jeremiah, to see how the ancient prophet's confidence in God's call helped him overcome his fears. Then Moises would share with them his own story—how his sense of the Holy Spirit's presence and leading made all the difference in his work of justice advocacy.

Moises' friends Fernando and Teresa Santillana returned from a missionary stint in Brazil, and Teresa was called to serve as a pastor for the Orangethorpe United Methodist Church. Knowing this would be a natural home for him, Moises began attending Teresa's church, and the long-time Catholic soon made a decision to become a Methodist. In 2003, Moises married Cecilia, a Salvadoran. He presently works for Clergy and Laity United for Economic Justice, and in 2007, helped kick off the New Sanctuary Movement (see Chapter 3). More than twenty-five years after the Sanctuary Movement around the wars in Central America, religious leaders from ten states joined together to start a new effort to protect immigrant families and to reform immigration policies that are tearing families apart. As an act of public witness, the New Sanctuary Movement invites congregations to provide hospitality and protection to select immigrant families whose legal cases revealed the contradictions and moral injustice of the current U.S. immigration system.

Even after all these years in the United States, Moises still has a longing in his soul to return to El Salvador, which he and Cecilia often talk about. In the meantime, however, he continues his faith-rooted justice organizing in southern California, carrying on his commitment to the biblical command to "love the immigrant as yourself."

5

House for *All* Peoples?
Reflections on Isaiah and Luke

Ched Myers

> *My House shall be called a house of prayer*
> *for all peoples. (Lk 19:46; Is 56:8)*

There is a unique kind of "trialectic" in the Bible regarding God's relationship to human beings, which moves between the universal and the "scandal of particularity." On one hand, the God of Creation cares for *all* peoples, exhibited in countless stories and teachings in both testaments. On a second hand, the God of Israel also calls and names a *peculiar* people (1 Pt 2:9), "formed by and for Godself" (Is 43:21), in order to nurture in them a distinctive way of life. On a third hand, the God of the Exodus clearly takes the side of poor and outcast people (of whatever tribe or tongue), being uniquely attuned to the "groans" of their suffering (Gn 4:10; Ex 2:24, 3:7).

The third characteristic of this trialectic guarantees the first: only by attending to the excluded can we truly realize the enfranchisement of all. And it is the vocation of the people called by the second characteristic to live in the tension of the first and third, seeking to love and serve all while at the same time allying with whosoever is forgotten or dispossessed in any given social context. Jesus of Nazareth embraced all three characteristics passionately: loving both national enemies and intimate betrayers, calling disciples, and living among the marginalized. But the roots of his vision of radical inclusion and solidarity are found a half-millennium earlier, in the writings of what appear to have been Jesus' favorite scriptures: the proclamations of a disciple of the great Israelite prophet Isaiah.

"Let Not the Foreigner Say . . ." Isaiah 56:1–8

Isaiah 56:1–8 is the opening stanza of the prophetic oracle sometimes referred to as "Third Isaiah." Second (Is 40–55) and Third Isaiah (Is 56–66) represent the work of successors to the eighth-century prophet (Is 1–39). Second Isaiah was probably composed during the exile of Israel's ruling classes to Babylon, Third Isaiah during the "reconstruction" period following their return to Palestine. These writings arose most likely from prophetic "schools," evidence of which we find in the Elijah/Elisha cycles (e.g., the "company of prophets" in 2 Kings 4:38). Here disciples carried on the work of their teachers, recontextualizing their word in another historical moment—which is, of course, what all preachers try to do every time they proclaim the Word to a community trying to practice their faith in time and space.

In his opening lines Third Isaiah sets a tone of radical inclusion, envisioning a time when people from all over the world, including ethnic outsiders and sexual minorities, will be welcomed as full members into God's house. This thesis is reiterated at the close of Third Isaiah: "The time has come to gather all the nations and tongues" (Is 66:18). *This* is the "new heaven and new earth" that YHWH intends to bring about (66:22).

Scholars date Third Isaiah sometime in the first two generations of the Israelite exiles' return from Babylon, between the reconstruction of the Temple (beginning in 515 BCE) and the time of Nehemiah (ca. 444 BCE). Persia, having defeated the Babylonians, was interested in sponsoring a client regime in Palestine for strategic reasons. Israelite exiles, for their part, wanted to rebuild Jerusalem and return to their positions of power, even if now constrained by their colonial overlords. This was a watershed time, and two key issues confronted the returnees. One was who would *lead* this social reconstruction project; the other was who would *participate* in it. Such questions shape any and all changing political landscapes.

Those who had been exiled to Babylon after the fall of Jerusalem were the urban elites of the former Israelite monarchy: priests, managers, the landed aristocracy, scribes, etc. The majority of peasants had remained in Palestine, working the land and scraping out a living, as the poor have always done under any regime. As the elites began to trickle back some fifty years after their defeat and deportation, they faced a dilemma. How would they reestablish their claims to land, to social status and to political position?

The returnees were a mixed bag, including land speculators and carpetbaggers trying to take economic advantage of the new settlements, priests determined to reestablish the cultic center as their power base, ultranationalists who saw a chance to rebuild old dreams of sovereignty, and political front men for Israel's new Persian imperial rulers who were trying to exert colonial control of the new entity in Palestine. But all of the elites agreed on one thing: *they* would define the reconstruction project, not the *am-ha-aretz* ("people of the land"; see Hammock 2000).

Such aspirations understandably generated conflicts with the existing population over property, politics, and religion. Many of those who had remained had enjoyed the fact that their former overseers were gone and had begun to shape autonomous indigenous traditions. The most dramatic point of conflict was the returnees' proposal to rebuild the destroyed Temple. King Cyrus of Persia, after intense lobbying by the exiles, had decreed that the returning Israelite leadership could reconstruct a temple in their homeland. This project was opposed by the *am-ha-aretz*, however, who didn't want to see a recentralization of local power. Cyrus' royal successor Darius halted construction for his own political reasons, and it took concerted efforts by Israelite elites to get Cyrus' original promise honored (a drama narrated in Ezra 1–9). One need only reference the situation in Palestine/Israel since 1948 to get a sense of the struggles between longtime residents on the land and ideologically motivated and politically powerful "returnees."

The strategy of the elites was to "divide and conquer" the peasantry by purging from the body politic those who did not conform to newly reasserted ethnic and purity standards. Their efforts to shore up the boundaries of the nation stressed genealogical integrity (advantaging the scribal class, who kept records of their lineage) and Levitical fidelity (advantaging the priestly class). The Persian overlords were supportive of such measures because an ethnically uniform colony was easier to manage politically, but the people of the land resisted these attempts to assert control.

The books of Ezra and Nehemiah reflect this preoccupation with defining insiders and outsiders, though the chronological question of which leader came first is a notoriously thorny one. But both agreed that marriage was the central focus for determining ethnic identity. Nehemiah allowed existing exogamous marriages to stand but forbade future ones, while Ezra took a more conservative position, instructing Judeans who had "married out" to divorce their foreign wives. (If Americans are tempted to feel morally superior toward such ancient statutes, we should remember that it was not until 1967 that the U.S. Supreme Court overturned a Virginia statute—replicated in fifteen other states—barring whites from marrying nonwhites, and Alabama did not remove it from its constitution until 2001!)

Ezra and Nehemiah's "reconstructionist" positions were legitimated on the basis of Deuteronomy 23:1–8, which specifically excludes "from the assembly" males who are not sexually functional, the "illegitimately" born, and foreigners (except Edomites and Egyptians). Similar laws are found in Leviticus 21:17–21, where physical disabilities disqualify a person for priestly service. We might call this the social strategy of "anthropological exclusion": ruling out persons not because of anything they have *done* but because of *who they are in their bodies/ethnicity.* We see this kind of logic misused repeatedly throughout the long and lamentable history of racist, patriarchal, and heterosexist ideologies and practices. And it continues to surface among some current anti-immigrant circles where it is assumed that most brown-skinned people are "illegals."

Third Isaiah argues vehemently against this position, taking specific issue with Ezra and Nehemiah's view that the nation would best be protected through "ethnic cleansing" and endogamy. Instead, Isaiah 56:1–8 calls for the boundaries of the community to be preserved through *ethical* behav-

ior. *Whoever* keeps the Sabbath, the text asserts, is entitled
to full inclusion. This point is underlined emphatically by
illustrating it with two "extreme" examples: eunuchs (het-
erosexually nonconforming males) and foreigners.

A dramatic opening line crystallizes the entire argument
to follow: "This is what God says: 'Maintain justice! Do
what is right! Then I will vindicate you!'" (Is 56:1). This
makes it clear from the outset that the issue is social justice,
not ritual or ethnic purity. Justice is immediately defined as
fidelity to Torah, keeping Sabbath and turning away from
evil (Is 56:2). Here the prophet is invoking the heart of the
ethical tradition of scripture. To keep Sabbath is to make
sure that everyone in the community has enough, and that
no one has too much; the gifts of the Creator must circulate rather than concentrate (Ex 16:16–19). "Sabbath Economics" prescribes practices designed to mitigate poverty
and social marginalization (such as debt release and gleaner's
rights) (Dt 15; Ex 23:10–12), and limits accumulation of
power and goods (see Myers 2001).

But Third Isaiah goes on to address specifically those
parts of the community that are being legally and socially
targeted:

> Let not the foreigner say . . .
> Let not the eunuch say . . .
> For *this* is what God says . . . (56:3f)

This verse seeks to animate the voices of those who
have internalized their rejection by the dominant culture
because of how they are perceived and publicly caricatured.
"The LORD will surely separate me from his people," says
the inner voice of the foreigner; "I am just a dry tree,"

intones the introjected contempt of the eunuch. Second-class citizens in our own history know all too well this self-hatred. Black children have tried to scrub their skin white, immigrants have changed their names, women have kept silent, and gays and lesbians have stayed deep in a destructive closet—all to avoid the contempt of a society that barely tolerates them. Internalized self-negation and external oppression are like a constant "acid rain," as psychologists William Grier and Price Cobbs famously put it in their landmark study *Black Rage* (1968). It is time, says Third Isaiah, for such dehumanization to stop—because YHWH says *otherwise*.

Commentators believe the prophet's rhetoric in Isaiah 56:4a implies a new ruling on case law, effectively overturning some of the Levitical strictures. The eunuch who holds to the Covenant will receive "in My house and within My walls, a monument and a name *better* than sons and daughters; I will give them an everlasting name that shall not be cut off" (Is 56:5). "Will not be cut off" (Heb *karat*) is a satirical play on the Hebrew word for eunuch (*saris*), which comes from an unused root meaning to castrate. This verb firmly links this oracle to the "new thing" YHWH is doing at the end of Second Isaiah: "Instead of the thorn shall come up the cypress . . . it shall be a memorial to the Lord, an everlasting sign that shall not be cut off" (55:13).

Eunuch occurs forty-two times in the Hebrew Bible, and is translated in Septuagint Greek as *eunouchos*, meaning "keeper of the bedroom," designating the role of royal eunuchs as chamberlains. There is continuing scholarly debate about whether this term narrowly refers to those who were emasculated to serve as court retainers or whether it is a broader term including all men who were socially

emasculated because of their sexual physiology or orientation. Matthew 19:12 suggests that there are *eunouchoi* made
by men and eunuchs "from birth," and I agree with those
scholars who believe that the latter clearly includes homo-
sexuals (see, e.g., Gaiser 1994). Third Isaiah knew very well
that eunuchs were, according to Leviticus, excluded from
cultic and family life. After all, since they couldn't procreate,
they could not reap the benefits of patrimony, including
land ownership. This also meant that their names would
be lost to posterity, an ancient way of rendering someone
socially and historically invisible. But YHWH insists instead
that eunuchs will have an honored place in the "House,"
something *better* than patrimony, symbolized by a special
"monument" and an "everlasting name." Playfully, the Hebrew word rendered as "monument" in the NRSV is *yad*,
usually translated as "hand" (cf. Is 57:8) but also as "power,"
"place," or as a euphemism for "penis"!

The prophet next addresses the only social group lower in the Levitical hierarchy than eunuchs: foreigners. He
repeats himself: if foreigners follow, serve and love God,
and observe Sabbath and Covenant, "I will bring them to
my holy mountain, and their sacrifices will be acceptable"
(56:6f). This is an extraordinary reversal of the ethnocentric
drift of Torah interpretation, both in the fifth century BCE
and since. In Third Isaiah's view, the Jerusalem Temple was
meant to be a world house, not merely a national shrine
like every other temple in antiquity. Its implications for our
contemporary view of immigration are profound.

Israel's house has been "repurposed," in order to be
"known as a place where all nations pray." This is Third Isaiah's answer to Ezra and Nehemiah's culture war on those
who didn't fit the ethnic-national ideal: don't force sexual
minorities out, and let foreigners in. YHWH welcomes

whosoever desires to follow the way, regardless of who they are in their somatic identity. But this vision did not prevail; the ethnocentric strategies of Ezra and Nehemiah carried the day. Indeed, some of those kicked out of the newly proscribed Judean body politic ended up as the despised Samaritans of Jesus' day. Chauvinism is powerful. Yet God's Word did not prove fruitless.

Remembering Prophetic Inclusion: Luke 4:16–30, 19:45f

More than four centuries later, Jesus of Nazareth dusted off that Isaiah scroll, looked hard at the synagogue audience one Sabbath day in his home town, and read, "The Spirit of the Lord is upon me, because God has anointed me to proclaim good news to the poor" (Lk 4:18f). When he was done citing Isaiah 61:1f—the heart of Third Isaiah —he added solemnly: "Today this scripture has been fulfilled in your hearing" (Lk 4:21). Jesus thereby announced a renewed campaign for inclusion rooted in *this* prophetic tradition.[1]

A little social and literary context helps us understand this scene. Nazareth is "where he had been brought up" (4:16), and its political geography is notable. Though the village was obscure, and otherwise unattested in ancient literature, it lay a mere three miles southwest of Sepphoris (also known as Zippori or Diocaesarea). Sepphoris had been built a century before Jesus on a Greek city plan and was later fortified by Herod the Great as the capital of Lower Galilee, complete with a theater and royal palace. After Herod's death in 4 BCE, a major Judean insurrection broke out, and the ancient Jewish historian Josephus tells us that one of the most important skirmishes was the sacking of the royal armory at Sepphoris, led by one "Judas, son of

Ezekias" (see *Antiquities,* 17:271 and *Wars* 2:56). In retaliation, Varus, the Roman legate of Syria, razed the city and sold the Jewish rebels into slavery.

Horsley and Silberman relate how Herod's son and successor Antipas moved shortly thereafter "to impose Roman Style order" on the region:

> Among his first acts was the establishment of a modern administrative center from which security forces, market inspectors, and tax collectors could be easily dispatched. The former regional capital of Sepphoris lay in ruins as a result of the recent uprising, and Antipas ordered that it be reconstructed as a modern Roman city with a palace, treasury, archives, and forum. When it was completed, he brought in a new population of loyal functionaries and workers—to replace the former inhabitants who had been killed by Varus's legions or sold off into slavery. He named the new city Autocratoris—literally . . . "belonging to the Emperor." (1997, 24)

If we assume that Jesus labored about fifteen years as a carpenter or construction worker (Gk *tekton*) in Nazareth, a one-hour walk from Sepphoris, then it is highly likely that he got work there rebuilding the city. The trauma of Sepphoris' destruction and reconstruction as a Roman city right at his doorstep would have had a profound impact on his consciousness, infusing in him a keen sense of the travails of empire—and doubtless the temptation to hate foreigners! This makes his inaugural sermon all the more remarkable.

Michael Prior (1995), in his exhaustive study of Luke's Nazareth sermon, points out that this scene is chiastic in structure:

A　And he came to Nazareth . . . and went to *the synagogue*

　　B　He *stood up* to read;

　　　　C　there was *given to him* the book of the
　　　　　　prophet Isaiah

　　　　　　D　*He opened the book* and found the place . . .

　　　　　　　　E　The *Spirit of the Lord* is upon me, because
　　　　　　　　　　God has anointed me

　　　　　　　　　　F　*to proclaim* good news to the poor

　　　　　　　　　　　　G　God has sent me to proclaim *release
　　　　　　　　　　　　　　to the captives*

　　　　　　　　　　　　**H　and recovery of sight to
　　　　　　　　　　　　　　the blind**

　　　　　　　　　　　　G' *to set at liberty* those who are oppressed

　　　　　　　　　　F' *to proclaim*

　　　　　　　　E'　the acceptable year of *the Lord*

　　　　　　D'　He *closed the book,*

　　　　C'　and *gave it back* to the attendant,

　　B'　and *sat down;*

A'　And the eyes of all *in the synagogue* were fixed on him.

This composition functions to emphasize Jesus' challenge to the "blindness" of his own people. The consecutive mention of the somatic "portals" of perception in the following verses (eyes, ears, and mouth; Lk 4:20–22) further underlines this theme. And the rhythm of standing, opening, reading, closing, sitting, and speaking renders this scene highly dramatic.

Scholars wonder whether Jesus chose Isaiah 61 or whether it may have been the *haftorah* from a lectionary for that day (4:17 could be interpreted either way).[2] There is also a running debate about the extent to which Jesus and his hearer would have understood the text's allusion to the "acceptable year" (Lk 4:19; Is 61:2a) in terms of the Jubilee tradition of debt release, land return, and slave manumission (on this, see Ringe 1985; Sloan 1977; Yoder 1994). What is clear is that Jesus' version of Isaiah's oracle omits the mention of YHWH's punishment of the enemy (Is 61:2b) and in his ensuing "sermon" emphasizes radical inclusion of foreigners in the promises of YHWH—a reading that almost gets him killed.

Luke 4:22–30 recontextualizes Third Isaiah in a way that was both challenging and risky. Jesus offers two *midrashic* illustrations of what *he* thinks Isaiah 61 meant, appealing to the two greatest Israelite prophets, Elijah and Elisha. Luke 4:25f alludes to the story of Elijah, an egalitarian Yahwist prophet, confronting Ahab in 1 Kings 17. Regarded as one of the worst of all Israelite kings (see 1 Kgs 21:25f), Ahab's wife worships Baal, and his officials have rebuilt the forbidden city of Jericho (16:31–34; see Jo 6:26).

Elijah battles the corrupt royal house by "conjuring" a drought (1 Kgs 17:1), invoking memories of Moses' battle with Pharaoh's empire by using natural disasters. The prophet is then sent by the Spirit to live in wilderness (17:2–6), just as both John the Baptist and Jesus are in Luke 3–4! While this "exile" suggests political marginalization, nature is clearly on the prophet's side, as Elijah is fed by ravens (see Lk 12:24). Ironically, however, the *wadi* by which Elijah settles dries up because of the drought, so God dispatches him to Zarephath, a Phoenician coastal village between Tyre and Sidon (1 Kgs 17:7–9). It is disturbing enough that Israel's prophet seeks refuge in the homeland of the dreaded Philistines; worse, Elijah seeks out a widow, straining propriety. Nevertheless, the two are hard pressed and help each other through the famine (17:10–16). This is the scandalous point that Jesus highlights in Luke 4:26: God dispatched Elijah to a *foreigner*, and they survived their respective crisis through cooperation. Luke's implication is that Jesus is *also* an embattled prophet who will stand in solidarity with "outsiders" while challenging the apostasy of the Judean elite (articulated in, e.g., Luke 10:29–37).

Jesus' second *midrash* concerns a story of Elisha (Lk 4:27; 2 Kings 5). Naaman is an Aramite general, who has been skirmishing with Israel. But this great warrior is a leper (an unlikely but key aspect to the story), and it is a captured Israelite slave girl who tells him about Elisha's capacity to heal. Namaan's subsequent encounter with the prophet (which completely bypasses Israel's king) is a hilarious parody: the Syrian initially acts contemptuously, disrespecting the Jordan River (2 Kgs 5:11f); he then yields to a ritual that is rife with Israelite symbolism (5:13f); and Elisha refuses to accept his payment, thus treating this enemy *foreigner* with compassion but also teaching him a lesson (5:15–19). This will also be Jesus' strategy in Luke's gospel: healing *and* confronting hubris.

In both "illustrative examples," Jesus challenges his audience's sense of exclusive ethnic entitlement by pointedly arguing that YHWH featured foreigners over Israelites in the work of their greatest prophets. Luke makes it clear that because of this, Jesus' synagogue audience quickly changed from admiration to hostility (Lk 4:28–30). The analogy of Martin Luther King's public speeches comes to mind: while many Americans loved his preacher's eloquence, they bristled when he dared to challenge the nation's persistent racism, militaristic nationalism, and entrenched poverty. Just as King was assassinated, so the Nazareth crowd sought to throw Jesus off a cliff (implying the punishment of a false

104 Our God Is Undocumented

prophet). But in Luke's story, "a prophet cannot perish away from Jerusalem" (13:33), so Jesus escapes.

The sharp moral of Jesus' inaugural sermon in Nazareth is, however, reiterated (in reverse order) in three consecutive episodes in Luke 7:1–17, as the following chart shows:

Luke 4:18–27	*Luke 7:2–22*
"to proclaim good news to the poor . . . recovery of sight to the blind"	c' 7:2–10: Foreign officer (centurion's servant) healed: "Not even in Israel . . ."
Elijah and widow of Zarapheth	b' 7:11–17: Widow of Nain ("a great prophet has arisen among us")
Elisha heals foreign officer	a' Tell John: "The blind see again . . . and the poor have good news proclaimed to them"

The sequence ends with Jesus' acknowledgment that his radically inclusive ministry is difficult: "Blessed is the one who is not scandalized by me!" (7:23).

The dramatic culmination of Jesus' struggle with the Judean authorities over his prophetic mission to the marginalized occurs in Luke's account of his "exorcism" (Gk *ekballein*) of the Jerusalem Temple (19:45f). To justify his action Jesus quotes directly from the Third Isaiah text studied above: "My House shall be called a house of prayer for all peoples" (Lk 19:46; Is 56:8). It is not overstating the case to say that Jesus, as portrayed by Luke, staked his entire vocation on the vision of Third Isaiah. Its ethos of radical inclusion animated his constant transgressions of social boundaries: eating with lepers, hanging out with women, touching the impure, teaching the excluded.

If Third Isaiah was so formative for Jesus, then, perhaps it ought also to guide us through the well-mined battlefields of our current culture wars. Third Isaiah's advocacy for faithful covenant-keeping over self-righteous gate-keeping is good news today, both to gay and lesbian Christians, who are having their discipleship dismissed, and to immigrants watching their civil rights erode. The biblical focus is upon *ethics*, not *anthropology*; or, as Dr. King famously put it, the issue is "the content of one's character, not the color of one's skin." Faithful discipleship (and responsible citizenship) is not about sexual orientation but social practice, not about what's on your passport but what's in your heart.

Unfortunately, our denominations prefer to approach these issues through studied ambivalence, interminable commissions, don't ask/don't tell avoidance, and repressive politeness. Meanwhile, many Christians tolerate or even engage in mean-spirited gay or immigrant bashing. The Christian Right has turned the war *on* terror abroad into a war *of* terror at home against those who don't fit the national ideal, lobbying hard to preserve the heterosexual monopoly on marriage and to militarize our borders. But the current conversation in our churches concerning both sexual minorities and undocumented immigrants would surely change if we took *this* Word of God seriously!

Third Isaiah and Jesus both call us to become a house of hospitality that reserves a special place for the otherwise excluded. Our communities of faith must be about discipleship, not disenfranchisement; communion, not exclusion.

Regardless of what *we* do, however, the God of justice will continue to welcome the outsider who wishes to follow and to warn erstwhile insiders that using God's name will *never* protect a "den of thieves" from judgment. May the church follow Jesus, who followed Isaiah, who followed YHWH, into a house for *all* peoples.

6

Proclaiming Liberty to the Captives: Amalia Molina

Matthew Colwell

In my Father's house there is lots of room. (Jn 14:2)

People of faith are challenged by Isaiah and Luke to welcome the excluded into that space that John's Jesus calls "my Father's House" in which "there is lots of room." It is hard to imagine a more ostracized and invisible group than immigrant detainees. Prison denies them access to crucial support structures of family, work, and legal protection. Ana Amalia Molina Guzman knew firsthand this kind of double marginalization, yet she emerged from her experience with a passion to proclaim the good news of God's care and justice to those facing the same ordeal.

Caught in the Web of Immigration Detention

Five-year-old Amalia heard a knock on her door. It was 1960 in San Salvador, and she was living with her father and younger brother, Francisco. Her parents were recently divorced, and her mother, Berta, was forbidden from visiting the father's home. So Amalia was surprised to open the door and see her mother standing there, asking, "Do you want to leave with me?" Amalia loved her father and was not eager to leave him. But she knew Francisco would choose to depart with their mother, and being separated from him was out of the question. "Yes," Amalia replied.

Berta brought the two of them to a house out in the country and asked her brother and his family to move in to care for Amalia and Francisco. She then began a vigorous battle to gain official custody of her children (divorce law in El Salvador automatically granted such custody to the father). She worked as a maid for one of the "fourteen families" in whose hands wealth and power was concentrated in El Salvador. With the help of that family's financial and legal support, Berta won custody a year later. The move to her mother's home, however, had not been a happy one for Amalia. She missed her father and her hometown neighbors, especially when celebrating *Las Posadas*; she felt like *she* was the stranger, and she broke down in the middle of the procession, sobbing inconsolably.

Berta worried for her daughter's mental health but also wanted to keep Amalia from being discovered by her father as the custody battle wore on. Less than a year after Berta had "kidnapped" Amalia, she sent her to a Catholic boarding school, where Amalia finally found the sense of home she had been yearning for. She felt security and predictability in being awoken at the same hour each day, told when to eat, and given a specific time to shower and brush her teeth. The nuns and the other children at the school were like a new family. When Amalia was twelve, her mother pulled her out of the boarding school, having long since won the custody battle. Amalia was devastated, and begged to return; a year later, Berta relented. Amalia remained at the school until she began her studies in public accounting at San Salvador's Jesuit University. After graduating, she went on to earn a master's degree in finance from the Technological University.

In December 1976, Amalia married Jose Gilberto Molina. Gil's father was determined to give all of his kids a command of English and an education in the United States, so he sent Gil to study at Louisiana State University on a student visa. After earning his degree in architecture, Gil returned to El Salvador to run a construction company. Amalia ran several small clothing boutiques, and the couple had three children: Diana Maria, Amalia Maria, and Jose Gilberto. But the political and economic turmoil of El Salvador's civil war in the 1980s took a toll on the family. Gil and Amalia were no longer able to get bank loans to sustain their respective businesses and took out private loans with exorbitant interest rates from unscrupulous moneylenders. To remain solvent, Gil's company took on government contracts to do work in San Vicente and Morazan—regions plagued by fighting. Many of these projects were funded by the U.S. Agency for International Development, and Gil's company was required to put out signs making this clear at construction sites, which made them targets for antigovernment guerillas. One of Gil's employees and his own brother were kidnapped, and his father shot in the head.

On one occasion, a housing project of Gil's was seized by the local union, and workers were ordered to strike. Gil had construction loans to pay back on the project, and as the strike continued, Gil's anxiety turned to desperation. Visits to the Department of Labor proved fruitless, so he decided to call a friend in the military to enlist his help. "The site has been shut down for over a month!" Gil lamented. "Don't worry about it," his friend replied. To Gil's dismay, he learned

his call had elicited a police and military intervention that
crushed the strike with tanks and multiple arrests. Gil had
now made himself an enemy of the union and would hence-
forth find it next to impossible to get contracting jobs.

The early 1990s brought the Salvadoran peace accords,
ending more than a decade of civil war. But it was still a
time of immense financial turbulence and political uncertainty, and for Gil, work was harder and harder to come
by. He and Amalia faced other challenges as well. Amalia learned Gil was having an affair with his secretary and
confronted him in 1994. Gil was repentant and sought to
disentangle himself from his personal relationship with this
secretary and from a joint business venture he had un-
dertaken with her. But as he did so, the family's financial
situation grew increasingly untenable. By 1995, with only
sporadic work, the interest they owed on private loans was
leading them to bankruptcy. The moneylenders often called
to threaten Gil, making him fear for his safety. Gil decided
to go to the United States

With help from friends and family, Gil pulled together
$5000 to give him a start in the United States, while Amalia
would stay in El Salvador, hoping to work out a settlement
with their creditors. Gil arrived in Los Angeles with a tourist visa and high hopes of starting a carpet cleaning business.
When that proved untenable, the only job this university-
trained architect found was selling blankets on the streets
of San Bernardino. Underemployment is a typical story for
immigrants of color, so when he learned of a job as the
Direct Assistance Program of the Gas Company, Gil jumped
at the chance.

Gil frequently called to plead with Amalia to join him
in the United States. With her family also pressing her to

go be with her husband, Amalia finally gave in. But before leaving El Salvador, she made one last effort to settle an outstanding debt. The moneylender, however, was unwilling to negotiate. Even though Amalia and Gil had paid back the original loan three times over, the lender insisted on continuing to compound monthly the exorbitant 5% interest. She hired a lawyer to negotiate with him, and leaving her three children with relatives, she went to join Gil. She was unaware that Gil's former secretary, angry at being dumped both as a lover and business partner, would seek out the moneylender; as she knew Gil's business affairs intimately, they hatched a plan to pursue the couple in the United States.

Amalia was disappointed to learn her new home was nothing but a garage in Baldwin Park, CA. When a realtor friend told them about a program for first-time buyers, they purchased a triplex with very little money down, moved into one of the units, and rented the other two. By the summer of 1997, they felt ready to have their three children join them. All three began school in the United States that fall. Meanwhile, Gil and Amalia pursued permanent residence; their lawyer thought they had a convincing asylum case, given the persecution and violence they had suffered in El Salvador. Things looked promising for the Molina family—but on March 18, 1998, their world turned upside down.

Amalia had just dropped her children off at school and was driving back home when an unmarked patrol car pulled her over. An officer handcuffed her, and she watched in horror as armed men with black jackets marked "Federal Police" surrounded her home. They rang the doorbell, and Diana, her nineteen-year-old daughter, answered. The federal agents barged in, arrested Gil, and searched the house. While Amalia was still waiting in the car, a man identifying himself as an immigration official asked for her passport, informing her that she and her husband had violated immigration laws by overstaying their visas. Amalia showed him documentation that she had applied for adjustment of status under paragraph 245i of the INS code, which granted immigrants the opportunity to negotiate residency while living in the country. The official dismissed the document and gave an order to have Amalia taken away. Before she left, Amalia was offered a moment—still in handcuffs—to give her purse to Diana. Seeing the terror in her daughter's eyes, Amalia told Diana not to worry but to take care of her younger siblings.

The officers took Amalia to an immigrant detention center in San Pedro. In the wake of the Illegal Immigration Reform and Immigrant Responsibility Act of 1996, immigrants—especially those who have had a past run-in with the law—could be placed in such centers indefinitely. In many cases, the only "crime" such immigrants had committed was fleeing torture and persecution in their home country and seeking asylum in the United States. For many, the detention center was merely a prelude to deportation; others were kept in an ill-defined holding pattern for months or even years. All were treated as prisoners, whether or not they had broken the law.

On the bus to San Pedro, Amalia's heart was racing, and her stomach felt like it had shriveled up into a ball; it was days before she could regain her appetite. Her greatest immediate fear was for her children, and she worried how these three inexperienced teenagers would cope in a new country without their parents. Once at the detention cen-

ter, Amalia and the other women were ordered to strip na-
ked and subjected to the humiliation and degradation of a
strip search, all on camera. They were then taken to a "pod,"
with a common bathroom, day room, and dorm room filled
with bunk beds. "Pod 6" would be her home not for a day
or two, but for the next sixteen months.

Amalia was locked up with over sixty other wom-
en ranging in age from eighteen to fifty-two, from Latin
America, Africa, China, India, Sri Lanka, France, Armenia,
Iran, and Syria. Many of the inmates were also mothers like
Amalia. Some were devastated to learn that when they were
deported, their U.S.-born children would be given up for
adoption, yet their confinement prevented them from fighting for custody. Amalia was issued a blue uniform, while Gil
was issued a red one in neighboring Pod 5. Though only
a concrete wall separated them, the two were forbidden to
communicate.

Amalia was told to take a free bunk bed and lay down,
feeling like she had been transported to another country. She
had imagined the United States as a land of freedom, justice,
and opportunity, but this was light years away from that image.
Powerless to help the ones she loved the most in the world,
her own children, she describes feeling "a gnawing pain that
presses against your chest, tears at your soul, and feels like a
slow death, because you have absolutely no options."

Keeping Faith in Pod Six

Like so many detainees, Amalia and Gil were not given a
court-appointed lawyer. They had no defined release date, no
educational opportunities, and were held in an overcrowded
and often dangerous environment. Temporary cots filled the

floor of the sleeping quarters, barely allowing room to walk. Though its capacity was seventy, Amalia counted as many as 125 inmates some days. Gang members were frequently brought in, and violence was commonplace. Amalia had to step in to break up fist fights, and Gil kept a coffee cup in his sock to defend himself from threats. Amalia was exposed to tuberculosis, and ultimately tested positive as a result of her time in Pod 6, though she did not contract the disease. Gil's health also deteriorated significantly in detention; though he received frequent X-rays, a cancerous tumor in his left lung went either undetected or unacknowledged by the medical staff. He did not learn about the tumor until a doctor noticed it after his release, by which time the cancer had grown and a crucial opportunity for treatment was missed.

This environment made it painfully clear to Amalia that she was considered little more than a number. Detainees were counted off three times a day, and the guards treated them like objects. They received just enough to keep them alive and to avoid legal problems with groups like Detention Watch Network, which monitors conditions of immigrant jails and advocates for the human rights of detainees. Amidst this dehumanizing environment, Amalia still found inspiration and the strength to persevere. One source of hope was the religious volunteers whom she met her very first Sunday in San Pedro. Outside for the morning recreation hour, she noticed a priest preparing to celebrate mass. Raised in Catholic schools and educated at the Jesuit University, Amalia found the presence of the priest a bright ray of hope and went over to join in. Tears poured down her face as she took communion, and after mass she introduced herself to Fr. Robert McChesney. A Jesuit who had spent time in Guatemala and El Salvador, Amalia made an immediate and powerful connection with him. She remembers the words he shared with her that day: "Amalia, there is great need here. Remember that your spirit is free."

Fr. McChesney later provided a tremendous gift to Amalia, arranging pastoral counseling sessions that brought her and Gil together. These were the only times she was able to meet with her husband during their time in detention. For Amalia, ministry groups from the different denominations were a tremendous source of support, making her feel loved and cared for, and reminding her she was accompanied by God and other compassionate human beings in her journey. She clung to her deeply held personal faith; though she occupied a hostile environment full of injustice and pain, she believed God had not abandoned her. When she went to court, she recited the prayer of Teresa of Avila: "Let nothing disturb you. Let nothing frighten you. Whoever has God lacks nothing." And she clung to the words of Isaiah 43: "Do not fear, for I have redeemed you; I have called you by name, you are mine. When you pass through the waters, I will be with you . . . when you walk through fire you shall not be burned, and the flame shall not consume you."

Amalia believed part of her role in the detention center would be "helping the other prisoners to overcome their fear, strengthen their faith, and find God's love in this place." She invited other cellmates to form groups to pray the rosary, and joined a Bible study that met every afternoon at 6 p.m., bringing together Catholics and Protestants to sing, study scripture, and share their stories. Looking back on her time in Pod 6, she believes it was her determination to help others that ultimately helped her maintain her identity and a sense of hope. Bilingual, she offered interpretive skills to the guards when they needed to converse with a detainee and helped people fill out forms, get doctor visits, and apply for asylum. She comforted women who cried out at night, plagued with nightmares, and wrote a letter to the judge on behalf of an ailing Mexican detainee who didn't speak English and longed to be reunited with her children. Amalia later learned that the four-sentence letter she wrote secured a court date for this woman, who was ultimately reunited with her children. Such acts earned Amalia the title "Mother Teresa." She tells members of her family today that when they feel weighed down with problems, they should try and find a way to serve others.

Amalia also found a great source of strength in her three children. Though she worried about them incessantly, she was determined to be reunited with them. At 5 a.m. each Sunday, the children would drive to San Pedro and line up for separate fifteen-minute visits with her. Amalia would challenge them to support one another and stay in school. "If you love me, show it," she told them; "take care of each other, and don't take drugs." But she and Gil recognized their children were in a tough situation. Amalia and Gil were unable to make mortgage payments from detention and didn't know how long it would be before the bank foreclosed. When first detained, they had only enough money in the bank for their children to get by for a month or so. They decided that to provide food for the kids, they would have to find a way to make some money while in detention. Gil learned to weave small wallets out of string, and Amalia learned how to make tiny ornaments from potato chip bags. By selling these handmade items, coupled with odd cleaning jobs, Amalia and Gil were able to pull together $50 a week. This allowed their children to purchase rice and beans, but little else.

The children felt terribly alone in the absence of their parents. Their home phone service was soon canceled when they couldn't make payments. Diana's boyfriend moved into the triplex, which proved disastrous when he tried to assume the "head of household" role, to the consternation of the two younger siblings. Over the course of their parents' sixteen-month detention, the bank repossessed the triplex, evicting the children. Diana had a job by that time as a parking valet and got an apartment with her boyfriend, but sixteen-year-old Amy and fourteen-year-old Jose refused to live with them. They accepted instead an offer from a single mother who Amy knew, who said the two could receive food and lodging at her home if they could provide child care for her two children. Amalia was sad to see the family further separated and insisted the three children stay in contact with one another.

Meanwhile, Gil and Amalia continued fighting a protracted legal battle. They learned their detention was a result of a warrant placed for their arrest with the international police. The moneylender in El Salvador, collaborating with Gil's former secretary, had claimed that Amalia and Gil had swindled them out of money. They had to defend themselves from this accusation while simultaneously making their legal case for political asylum. Through the course of this legal drama, they came close to being deported back to El Salvador. Eventually their lengthy legal fight proved successful, and the criminal charges were dropped. On July 26, 1999, Gil and Amalia were released.

But the couple had no home to return to; the triplex and all of their possessions had been repossessed by the bank. Their first night of freedom was spent sleeping in Diana's apartment on a mattress Amy had found lying out in the street. But all five family members had survived the ordeal and were back together in Diana's apartment. Diana and Amy both had jobs, and Amy and Gil Jr. both offered to drop out of school to help support the family. But Amalia learned how difficult the ordeal had been for them and insisted that they finish their studies.

Amalia applied for a work permit, but since her legal case had not yet reached a resolution, the request was initially denied. Still, she considered ways she might serve others, recalling the impact that religious volunteers had on her and the other inmates at the detention center. They brought the good news of God's love and showed by their compassion that the inmates were not mere numbers, but children of God. Yearning to extend that kind of care to others, Amalia started volunteering at Los Padrinos, a juvenile hall in Downey, CA. There was a wing for undocumented immigrant children, many of whom had been looking for their parents at the border when they were picked up by authorities. Most of these children didn't speak English and found themselves teased by the others. Since many of the guards only spoke English too, they felt quite isolated and terrified. Amalia focused her visitation ministry on these children, since her experience gave her an acute sense of the struggle they were facing. Her trips to Los Padrinos allowed her not only to reach out to others in need, but to gradually repair her own self-esteem.

Good news arrived the first spring after her and Gil's release. They had been granted political asylum, putting an end to a long chapter in their immigration saga. They acquired green cards, and Gil was able to get a commercial truck driver's license. Amalia made plans to sell real estate. But then bad news arrived regarding Gil's health: he had lung cancer. He spent the ensuing months battling the disease, but he succumbed in the summer of 2001, almost two years after his release from San Pedro. Before his death, Gil made it clear to his children he did not want them returning to El Salvador. "The law is not perfect here," he told them, "but they will fix this. That's what I like about this country—you can fix things here."

Gil's death hit Amalia hard. It was a struggle for her to keep going, and her children worried she was depressed. She spent all her nonworking hours in front of the television and was reluctant to go out. But she maintained the visitation ministry at Los Padrinos, and her volunteer work was getting noticed. The Jesuit Religious Service (JRS) observed Amalia's compassion for others, and offered her a job as an office assistant. She took it, recalling a vow she had made in San Pedro that if she was released, she would denounce the injustices she had observed while behind bars. She promised herself she would be a voice for those inside who had been silenced. And as she spoke with others on the outside, she became aware of how little people knew of what was occurring in the detention centers.

She had kept in touch with Fr. McChesney after she was released, who encouraged her to write a book about her experience. Pulling together some personal notes she had taken during her time there, she wrote *The Power of Love: My Experience in a U.S. Immigration Jail* (2003). As a result, Amalia began receiving invitations to speak, and she shared with various groups what was happening inside immigration detention centers. After she had worked with JRS for five years, the Los Angeles Catholic Archdiocese asked Amalia to help with their "Get on the Bus" program, which brought children from throughout California to visit their mothers in prison on Mother's Day. In many cases, this visit was the only time they got to see one another, as the children were often cared for by relatives who lacked the financial means or the transportation to get to a distant prison.

Later the Archdiocese asked Amalia to coordinate a "Families of the Incarcerated" program, one of its restorative justice ministries. She continues this work today, involving visiting detention facilities, leading educational seminars, and bringing in lawyers to provide free legal advice to prisoners. One of its initiatives is "Journeys of Hope," an effort to connect children with their imprisoned parents. It focuses on facilitating a final visit between immigrant parents facing deportation and their children. Amalia is acutely aware that these parents will never see their children again, so the meetings can provide a crucial sense of closure. The children can realize they were not intentionally abandoned but victims of laws that their parents were powerless to fight. In her education seminars, Amalia stresses to incarcerated immigrants the importance of preparing for the possibility of deportation, whether or not they believe it will happen.

Amalia runs retreats and healing services for family members who have a loved one behind bars. She knows what it is like to be an inmate, and Amalia longs to be a presence of care and accompaniment for others facing such circumstances. As meaningful as this volunteer work is, she acknowledges that it is not for everybody. Many volunteers who see the conditions inmates must endure want to speak out for change, but if they challenge detention center authorities, they often lose their visiting privileges. It is difficult for religious volunteers to limit their support to prayer, words of compassion, and empathy. For those wishing to advocate for more just and humane conditions for those incarcerated, Amalia commends the aforementioned Detention Watch Network and Families of the Incarcerated, which has resources and programs to support those behind bars.

Amalia's pursuit of justice on behalf of immigrant detainees, and affirmation of their full humanity through ministries of compassion, embodies the vision of radical inclusion urged by Third Isaiah and Jesus. Even for those in detention, there is room enough in God's house.

7

"Nothing from Outside Can Defile You!" Jesus' Embrace of the "Other" in Mark 4–8

Ched Myers

And he saw that they were making headway painfully, for the wind was against them. (Mk 6:48)

The deep, collective anxieties fueling anti-immigrant sentiment in the United States today arise from many factors, but certainly one has to do with an inchoate fear of racial-cultural difference. There is considerable irony in the fact that for "white" culture, which is exclusively made up of persons whose ancestors were immigrants, contemporary immigrants are perceived as "other." Fear of this otherness is, of course, usually coded in expressions of concern about health, criminal justice, the capacity of public institutions, or cultural or religious differences (a discourse often tinged with racial caricature). But at the root of alarmist polemics by so-called nativist political movements are allusions to issues of what anthropologist Mary Douglass called "purity" and "danger" (1966). Such groups believe that enforcement, even to the point of militarization, of our borders is necessary to protect not only economic or social entitlements, but indeed the very *integrity* of the body politic.

It is endemic to human nature that social groups establish boundaries in order to determine who is "in" and who is "out." Sometimes these borders are natural, such as rivers or mountains. Sometimes they are constructed, physical impediments, such as fences or fortresses. And sometimes they are symbolic boundaries, articulated through defining cultural practices, such as a style of dress, a particular diet, or a linguistic system.

Natural and constructed boundaries that keep people apart can be a good thing—especially when they help protect weaker individuals or groups from domination by those who are stronger. Three examples suffice to make this point. In the long, bloody history of western colonization, indigenous peoples all over the world suffered greatly from the fact that their "borders" (which were usually symbolic and customary) were ignored by aggressive, well-armed Europeans intent upon expropriating lands and resources. The two-hundred-mile exclusive economic zone (established at the Third United Nations Convention on the Law of the Sea in 1982) represents a boundary that helps small coastal nations preserve a measure of economic self-determination. And a fence around a primary school serves to provide some protection for young children.

This "defensive" function of borders is almost always cited as justification for their establishment and enforcement. More often, however, it is the strong who put up boundaries to protect their structural advantages and privileges from the weak. The borders of powerful nations or institutions often function rather to impose inequality and even to render disenfranchised groups invisible. Three examples would be the militarized zone at the U.S.-Mexico border, gated communities in suburban areas, and the fortress architecture of downtown corporate offices.

In scripture we find evidence of boundaries that protect the vulnerable from the predatory such as "cities of refuge" (Nm 35; Dt 19) or the "law of gleaner's rights" (Lv. 19:9f; see Ex 23:9–12). The former protected an unconvicted manslaughter from blood vengeance, while the latter stipulated that the edges of every field should remain available to "the poor and the sojourner," a part of the wider "Sabbath Economics" code in Torah that delimited proprietary ownership in order to ensure that the landed classes were not privatizing the commonwealth (see Myers 2001). On the other hand, boundaries that insulate the powerful from the weak are challenged by biblical faith.

We see this nowhere more clearly than in Mark's gospel chapters 4–8, where Jesus defies both customary and geographic boundaries in order to engage with the social and political "others" of first-century Roman Palestine, specifically to include gentiles in his ministry of healing and provision. Not only does Jesus pointedly teach that external borders *cannot* guarantee the integrity of a body politic, he also models how to "shed" the ideology of in-group entitlement for the sake of God's dream of inclusion.

"Let Us Go Across to the Other Side" The Dangerous Journey of Boundary Crossing

The evangelist Mark, otherwise the sparest of our gospel narrators, waxes curiously redundant in the second major section of his story. There are two perilous crossings of the Sea of Galilee during storms (Mk 4:35–41, 6:45–53), two feedings of hungry masses in the wilderness (6:33–44, 8:1–9), and two pairs of healings (5:21–43, 7:24–37). The purpose of this repetitive composition is to articulate two roughly parallel "cycles" of ministry, each taking place on different sides of the sea, which Jesus and his disciples are traversing in boat trips back and forth throughout this sequence.

The Sea of Galilee, the key topographical feature of northern Palestine, is the narrative center of gravity in the first half of Mark. The first disciples are called (1:16–20, 2:13) and taught there (3:7, 4:1ff). In Mark 4:35, Jesus and his disciples embark on the first of several journeys to "the other side" of the sea, an area equated in the story with everything east of the Jordan (see 3:8, 10:1). From Mark's point of view, this is hostile territory, symbolizing everything alien and threatening to the Jewish population west of the sea. There are four "crossing journeys" in Mark 4–8: three boat voyages and a circuitous trip by land to foreign regions:

- 4:35f–5:1f: voyage from Capernaum to the Decapolis (return 5:21);
- 6:45–6:53: voyage to Bethsaida that disembarks at Gennesaret (blown off course?);
- 7:24–7:31: land journey to foreign coastal cities of Tyre and Sidon, returning via the Decapolis;
- 8:10, 13: voyage from Dalmanutha to Bethsaida (arrive 8:22).

The function of this crossing pattern is to dramatize the fact that Mark's Jesus is determined to bring liberation to those on the "other side," despite their cultural and political differences. It is a systematic transgression of borders for the purposes of human solidarity. Let's look a bit closer.

Upon conclusion of his parables sermon, Jesus invites his disciples to set sail for "the other side" (4:35). But a storm blows up, and the boat begins to take on water (4:37). The disciples, among whom are experienced fishermen, realize they are going down. In a moment of high pathos, they scream at their dozing leader: "Master, do you not care if we perish?!" (4:38). Jesus then rebukes the storm (4:39). Mark's story alludes to Psalm 107:23–30; however, it ends not with relief or triumph but with mutual doubt:

Jesus: "Do you not yet have faith?" (4:40).
Disciples: "Who then is this that even the sea and wind obey him?" (4:41; cf. 1:27).

Indeed, the disciples are more unnerved *after* Jesus silences the storm than they were in the midst of it (4:41)! Is this due to their awe before a "nature miracle," or to their dread of actually having to complete this border crossing? We can answer this by seeing how this boat story (and its counterpart in 6:45–52) draws on archetypal symbols.

Mark consistently refers to the freshwater lake as a "sea" in order to invoke the most primal narratives in Hebrew tradition: the Ark of Noah and the crossing of the Red Sea. But above all he is drawing here on the tale of Jonah, the prophet who resisted the call to preach to a foreign enemy (see Jon 1). This prophet fled from his mission because he was unconcerned with the fate of those suffering oppression under the Assyrian imperial city-state of Nineveh (4:11). He is thus caught up in a "great storm" (1:2–4)— just like the disciples in Mark's story.

Mark's drama at sea is curious; after all, veteran fishermen would have been neither surprised nor intimidated by a storm on the Sea of Galilee. Symbolically speaking, however, the wind and waves represented cosmic forces of opposition in the Bible (see, e.g., Ps 104:7). Thus in Mark the storm symbolizes everything that impeded a Jew's attempts to cross geopolitical and cultural boundaries to "the other side." The enmity between Jew and gentile was seen by most of Mark's contemporaries as the prototype of all human hostility, and the separation between them considered part of the "natural order." The harrowing sea stories suggest that the task of social reconciliation was not only difficult, but virtually inconceivable. Yet Jesus "stills the storm" to make *this* journey possible.

In contrast to Jonah, Jesus embraces the task of engaging an imperial adversary with the good news of liberation. His crossing takes him to the vicinity of the Decapolis (Mk 5:1). This region was settled by many veterans of the Roman military conquest of Palestine (land taken as spoils) and thus represented an imperial zone resented by nationalist Jews. It is telling that Jesus here confronts a powerful demon named "Legion," whom he vanquishes in a manner distinctly reminiscent of another anti-imperial tale—the drowning of Pharaoh's soldiers in the Sea (5:2–20; see Ex 14). The demoniac's restoration "to his right mind" strongly suggests that this story means to portray "possession" as a symbol (or symptom!) of the land's military "occupation" by Rome (on this see Myers 2008, 190ff).

All this conflict and drama explains why in Mark's second boat episode, Jesus must *force* the disciples to make the crossing (6:45)! For a second time we find the hapless fishermen upon a raging sea in the dead of night, straining pitiably against roaring headwinds (6:47f). Mark says they were "tortured at the oars," yet losing ground. Is there a more heartbreaking portrait of the struggle of discipleship against the stream of history?

Jesus' walk on the sea is a moment of revelation that the disciples miss, thinking he is a "ghost" (6:48f). When they realize it is him, they are profoundly "agitated," suggesting that the storm now rages *inside* them as well. Now comes the response to their frightened question that concluded the first boat trip ("Who is this?"; 4:41). Jesus identifies himself as the "I AM" (6:50), an extraordinary invocation of the name of YHWH (see Ex 3:4). Mark's good news is that the God of Exodus *still* meets us as we embark on the risky journey toward true freedom.

But in the realism of Mark's story, the disciples are "beside themselves" (Mk 6:51), and this second crossing is unsuccessful (6:53). The disciples have contracted "Pharaoh's disease": their hearts are hard, and they cannot understand the purpose of these voyages, which Mark alludes to in terms of "loaves" (6:52). This metaphor will reoccur in the final boat story of this section (8:11–21), where it is revealed that Jesus' sea crossings and wilderness feedings have been for the purpose of creating "only one loaf" of human solidarity (8:14). But there are yet more object lessons to come before Mark reveals this extraordinary "punch line."

"Do You Fail to Understand?"
Parables of Political Bodies and the Body Politic

Following hard on the heels of Mark's second boat crossing is a curious and often overlooked teaching section (7:1–23). It addresses directly the inevitable anxiety that "in-groups" experience when contemplating any sort of interaction with "out-groups." Jesus' instruction is presented explicitly as a parable that disciples (then and now) must be *sure* to understand and is followed with an illustrative object lesson so we won't miss the point (7:24–30).

The scene opens with Jesus being challenged by local authorities to defend his disciples' practice of sharing table fellowship with "unclean" persons, referring here to lower-class members of the Judean society (7:1–5). The set-up presents a revealing contrast between Jesus and the Pharisees by comparing their respective relationships to the poor who typically inhabit the public town square:

- Wherever Jesus went into villages or cities or the countryside, they laid the sick in the marketplaces (Gk *en tais agorais*) and begged Jesus that they might touch even the fringe of his cloak; and all who touched it were healed (6:56).
- When the Pharisees return from the marketplace (Gk *ap' agorās*), they do not eat anything unless they ritually purify themselves (or it) (7:3f).

This emphasis on contamination in public space and the "politics of touch" anticipates another Markan engagement with the Purity Code.

What follows is a three-part episode:

- 7:1–5: The Pharisees challenge Jesus' disciples; explanation of the purity issues involved;
- 7:6–13: Jesus counterattacks Pharisaic authority;
- 7:14–23: Jesus returns to the original issue of meal sharing, offering a "parable."

The question here is whether table fellowship—so fundamental to the social fabric of life in ancient Mediterranean culture—should mirror restrictive group boundaries or expand them.

Mark's Jesus has already skirmished with the authorities concerning who, when, where, and what is appropriate concerning eating (2:15–28). Now the issue is "how": apparently Jesus' disciples have been following his example of ignoring certain purification rites at table (7:2). Washing of hands, produce, and utensils had nothing to do with hygiene in this cultural context, but with the symbolic removal of impurity (7:3f). In Pharisaic Judaism, such habits, together with kosher dietary rules, functioned to enforce social boundaries in two ways. Politically they helped define ethnic identity (in a context where most folk looked and dressed alike); socially, who one ate with and what one ate reflected one's status in the class hierarchy.

The fact that Mark sets this debate in relation to the marketplace suggests an economic dimension in the background as well. Pharisaic regulators oversaw whether food had been rendered unclean at some stage of production or distribution. For example, was seed sown on the Sabbath,or fruits harvested without properly separating out tithes? Many Galilean peasants resented the attempts of these "middlemen" to control the food economy (for more on this, see Myers 2008, 47ff, 157ff, 217ff). Thus in this "policing" incident, the Pharisees were, in effect, accusing the disciples of group disloyalty, while defending their own status as economic and cultural brokers. Moreover, they charge Jesus' community with ignoring the "tradition of the elders" (Mk 7:5). This was a body of legal interpretation that the Pharisaic movement claimed had been handed down orally alongside the written Torah.

Jesus moves from defendant to prosecutor by refusing to recognize the authority of their "human tradition," contrasting it with the "commandment of God" (7:8f). He then appeals to Isaiah to underline his "scripture first" position (Mk 7:6f; Is 29:13), an oracle that denounces false prophets (29:10) and people who "cannot read" (29:12). Then Jesus invokes a bit of "case law" (Mk 7:9f), arguing that Torah enjoins a responsibility to provide economic support for one's aging parents (see Ex 20:12). Jesus accuses the Pharisees of circumventing this obligation by allowing (presumably wealthy) people to dedicate their estates to the Temple (the meaning of *korban*, Mk 7:11). Such vows froze a family's assets until at death they were released to the Temple treasury (for which they represented an important source of revenue). But because this practice leaves the dependent elderly financially ostracized, the pious "vow" to the Temple becomes in fact an economic "curse" upon the aged (7:12), thus "nullifying the command of God" (7:13; see Ex 21:17).

The principle articulated here is that the needs of the vulnerable trump the demands of institutions—not to mention the sophistry of the privileged. It is demonstrated in other Markan conflict stories as well (e.g., Mk 5:21–43 and 12:38–44, which directly indicts the Temple treasury in the exploitation of the poor). Mark's Jesus insists that when religious practices function to legitimate social inequities, they subvert justice.

Jesus concludes the episode with a signal to the reader to pay careful attention to the "moral" of this story: "Listen to me all of you, and understand" (7:14). He now issues a parable: "There is nothing outside you that by going in can defile you; only that which comes out of you can defile" (7:15). This mysterious trope is immediately decoded for the Twelve in the following household scene (7:17): the physical body is a symbol of the "body politic" of Israel.

This was a common political analogy in antiquity and is also employed by the Apostle Paul (see 1 Cor 12:12ff).

Jesus' point is that the social boundaries constructed by the Purity Code are powerless to protect the integrity of the community, which can only truly be "corrupted" by its own flawed character. Taking a page from Third Isaiah's argument (see Chapter 5), Jesus concludes that the true "site of purity" is not the body but the *heart*, the moral center in Hebrew anthropology (Mk 7:18–20). A vice list follows, alluding in part to the prophet Hosea's denunciation of public crime in Israel: theft, adultery, and murder (7:21; Hos 4:2). Jesus has redrawn the lines of group identity: the class and ethnic "fence" of purity observance is replaced by the rigor of collective ethical self-scrutiny.

Mark parenthetically interprets Jesus' teaching here to mean that "all foods are clean" (Mk 7:19)—a central, if controversial, conviction of the earliest Jewish church. Not only does this edict reenfranchise marginalized Jews who were unable to conform to the demands of purity, it also suggests that a kosher diet must no longer function to proscribe table fellowship with non-Jews! Mark thus agrees with both Luke (see Acts 10:9–16) and Paul (see Rom 14) that obstacles to building community with ethnic outsiders must be removed—no matter how fundamental they might seem to one's own culture!

This may be at once Jesus' most radical and widely ignored teaching. It rejects all external boundaries as impotent to protect one's community from perceived threats from the race and class "other." Excluding or insulating ourselves from outsiders *cannot* protect us or our character —only our own ethical behavior can do that. We should not underestimate how radical Jesus' proposition was for a first-century Jew. And for modern North Americans? An analogy might be to redefine U.S. citizenship not by one's legal documents but by one's genuine commitment to the Bill of Rights: an ethical ideology of "open borders"!

Having "told" this principle, Jesus now proceeds to "show" it (if somewhat ironically) the very next episode. Having earlier in the story presented a healing doublet in "Jewish" territory (Mk 5:21–43), Mark now narrates a corresponding doublet in "Gentile" territory (7:24–37). Jesus journeys to the region of Tyre and Sidon, a coastal region northwest of Galilee considered outside the scope of Palestinian Jewish society. Indeed, it was the homeland of Israel's historic enemies, the Phoenicians (a.k.a. Philistines; 7:24a). These healings will serve as dramatic object lessons in the radical inclusivity just advocated.

The woman who falls at Jesus' feet appealing on behalf of her off-stage daughter (7:25f) reminds us of Jairus (5:22f), but represents a world remote from that of the synagogue leader. Because we are unfamiliar with what constituted social propriety in Hellenistic antiquity, we miss the scandal of this encounter. In conventional Mediterranean honor culture it would have been inconceivable for an unknown, unrelated woman to approach a man in the privacy of his "retreat." Worse, here is a gentile soliciting favor from a Jew. Mark's description is emphatic: she is "Greek, a *Syrophoenician* by birth" (7:26).

This affront explains Jesus' initial rebuff, which churchly readers often find troubling (7:27). He responds in a manner that would have been expected from a Jewish male, defending the collective honor of his people by rebuffing her sharply. We cannot sugarcoat the fact that Jesus is *insulting* this woman. "Doggie" was a popular Jewish epithet for gentiles; a rabbinic saying of the time asserted that "he who eats with an idolater is like one who eats with a dog" (see also Ex 22:31). Jesus' stipulation that "the children must first be satisfied" intones a conventional Jewish sense of primacy.

Jesus' eating metaphor is boldly turned back upon him by the woman, however, in her surprising and brilliant retort: "Yes lord, but even the dogs under the table eat the crumbs meant for the children" (Mk 7:28). Protocol has now been strained to the breaking point as she dares to challenge this rabbi. Yet she, too, is only defending the rights of her people to "the table." The real jolt, however, is the story's conclusion. Jesus, who has and will master in verbal riposte every other opponent in Mark's story, here *concedes* the argument: "Because of your teaching (Gk *logon*) . . . the demon has left your daughter" (7:29)!

In the narrative logic of Mark, she has reminded him of his own assertions regarding inclusion made in the previous episode! Interpreters debate whether Jesus should be understood here to have been in the wrong or having "allowed" himself to be corrected in order to make the exchange into an object lesson. But the payoff is the same: his dignity as a Jewish male has severely been affronted by a gentile woman who "bests" him. This, however, is precisely the problem with honor culture, then and now: it requires winners and losers. This story seems to model a different approach. The collective honor of Jesus' people is no longer the ultimate value; rather, fundamental *human* solidarity is more important, including embracing persons furthest from one's own group.

Of course, when traditional social boundaries are opened to welcome the "other," the in-group inevitably perceives itself as having been diminished, unable to see or embrace

the bigger vision. A dramatic example would be the frustration and rage experienced by slave-owning whites in the
South with the end of slavery in the 1860s, and again with
the managers of Jim Crow after desegregation in the 1960s.
It felt like a loss of identity (however disfigured by ideologies of racial superiority).

Mark wishes to show a way through this "indignity" to
deeper liberation. So Jesus, the Jewish male, conspires with
an importune female foreigner in an encounter that ends
with a radical redistribution of power. He is modeling what
we might call the "cost of discipleship," in the conviction
that the short-term pain of losing face will be eclipsed by
ultimate goal: that *all* God's children be "satisfied." And in
Mark's story, that dream is symbolically realized in Jesus'
wilderness feedings on both "Jewish" *and* "gentile" sides of
the sea (the Greek verb "to satisfy," *chortazō,* is used in 6:42,
here in 7:27, and again in 8:4,8). In Mark 7 Jesus has both
taught and demonstrated the divine economy of enough
for everyone, which transcends and transforms even our
most dearly held individual or group entitlements.

Mark, the realist, rightly anticipated that this radical message would fall on deaf ears. So this sequence moves to the
healing of a gentile man unable to speak or hear. This episode occurs back in the Decapolis, that archetypal "territory
of the enemy" where the Roman "Legion" was exorcised
(5:9, 20), the endpoint of Jesus' long itinerary that symbolically embraces all the gentile territory surrounding Galilee
(7:31). Here is one more object lesson in which an alienated "political body" is made whole in order to advance the
restoration of a wider and inclusive "body politic."

But though Jesus can liberate the mute (7:37; see Is
35:5f), his own disciples remain "deaf" to the *logos* of the

Syrophoenician woman and "blind" to the mystery of the loaves (see Mk 8:18). This irony refocuses the narrative on the heart of Jesus' mission: to move his own people from denial to discipleship. Mark thus concludes the first half of his gospel with Jesus' stern warning to his followers—delivered on their last boat crossing—to "beware of the leaven of the Pharisees and of the Herodians" (8:15). That is to say, we must learn to discern and resist the social and political forces of exclusion that will always jeopardize the "one loaf" around which the church is called to gather (8:16–21).

When boundaries function to defend privileges of the "haves" from the desperation of the "have-nots," the Bible takes sides on behalf of the excluded. Jesus models a way that transgresses borders, embraces the "other," and embodies the dream of God by welcoming everyone to the table. These gospel stories remind us that challenging the social protocols of simple table fellowship can change the world. When four young African American college students sat down at a Woolworth's lunch counter on February 1, 1960, they began a nonviolent revolution that spelled doom for the persistent system of American apartheid. We should never underestimate the power of a strategic meal—especially when it is shared across boundaries.

The task of our churches, at once both pastoral and prophetic, is to help citizens who are anxious about preserving the body politic to see that external borders can't protect us. Quite the contrary: risking communion with the "political bodies" of immigrants might just save us. As the next chapter shows, John Fife, a Presbyterian pastor in Tucson, AZ, summoned the courage to embrace the kind of gospel faith that defies borders in order to rediscover human solidarity. Amidst the current culture war waged around the world against these vulnerable populations, we all need to "hear and understand" Jesus' teaching again (7:14). If we exclude or criminalize today's outsiders, we too are "without understanding" (7:18a). But Jesus has the power to restore *our* perceptions.

8

Reimagining the Underground Railroad: John Fife

Matthew Colwell

Your loins girded, your sandals on your feet, and your staff
in your hand, you shall eat this meal in haste. (Ex 12:11)

The Sanctuary Movement offers a powerful and enduring example of people of faith who embraced Jesus' challenge to cross to "the other side" at a critical moment in
American history (see Chapters 3 and 7). Jesus' teaching
that "there is nothing outside you that can defile you" (see
Chapter 7) became a core conviction of one of the movement's founders, Pastor John Fife. To Rev. Fife and his colleagues, undocumented "outsiders" were not a source of
defilement for the American body politic. Rather, they represented an invitation to deeper human solidarity, so he and
his Sanctuary colleagues made costly commitments to the
refugees in exodus from Central America's U.S.-sponsored
wars, accompanying them "in haste" on their journey to-
wards freedom.

John's thirty-five year ministry of transgressing social
and political borders began worlds away from Arizona's

border war zone. It started in Pennsylvania at seminary in the summer of 1963. "Sign me up!" was Fife's response when asked to join a group of students and faculty from Pittsburgh Theological Seminary for a road trip to the South. "It beats the hell out of studying Greek." So began a journey to the March on Washington for Jobs and Freedom, spearheaded by Dr. Martin Luther King, Jr., and the civil rights movement, which would prove galvanizing for Fife and the country.

From Seminary to the Streets

John grew up in small-town western Pennsylvania where the white, middle-class Presbyterian Church of his youth played the role of defending the status quo rather than challenging social norms. But his seminary studies, coinciding with the emerging civil rights movement, provided Fife with a stirring new model of what it could mean to be church. He saw faith communities providing the spiritual underpinning of a broad movement for social justice that was transforming the nation. Studying under professors like Markus Barth and Gayraud Wilmore, John learned the many connections between the gospel and the "Movement." He began understanding the message of Jesus Christ as a call to end systems of exclusion and oppression in favor of radical inclusion for those who had been kept marginalized —and saw this enacted in the civil rights struggle. If he was going to take Christ seriously, he concluded, he had to be an active part of organizing for change.

Though at the August 1963 march John was assigned the unglamorous task of trash detail, he was thrilled to be in the midst of that historic moment. He soon joined other student and faculty trips to the Poor People's March in Washington, DC, and to Birmingham, AL. He also became involved in civil rights efforts locally, partnering with an African American Presbyterian church on the North Side of Pittsburgh that was spearheading a local desegregation campaign. John joined in picketing the suburban homes of slum landlords, calling them to pay attention to the squalor in which their tenants were living.

John was also impacted by the message of nonviolence that King and others in the civil rights movement were proclaiming, which he perceived to be in line with Christ's call to love one's enemy. As the conflict in Vietnam escalated, he took part in antiwar efforts, heading again to Washington, DC, as a part of a seminary delegation that would soon form Clergy and Laity Against the War. John became increasingly convinced that his faith called him directly into the throes of social change work, which he believed could bring about real results.

It was a love interest, however, that lured John away from Pennsylvania to the place where his life's work of pastoral ministry and faith-based organizing would find a home. After he began his seminary studies, Marianne, whom John had been dating since college, transferred to Arizona University to be closer to her family. John started researching summer internships in Arizona and soon got a call inviting him to work at a Tucson Indian Reservation. The caller asked if he had any questions. "Just two" John replied. "What's an Indian, and what's a reservation?"

The caller explained that although the churches had done a lot of damage to Native Americans over the years, he figured that over the course of a three-month summer internship John probably couldn't do a whole lot more.

John signed up and that summer found his heart and spirit captured by the Southwest. He fell in love with the Tohono O'odham people and the stark beauty and spirituality of the landscape. He enjoyed not only being close to the border of Mexico, but far from western Pennsylvania. The Fifes could trace their family history there to immigrant ancestors who arrived from Scotland and Northern Ireland in the 1760s. Four of the past five generations had been Presbyterian pastors, including John's father. Knowing he would soon become yet another Rev. Fife, John was eager to move far from his home state.

John and Marianne were married in 1967, but as his graduation neared, he was unable to find a single church in the Southwest with a pastoral vacancy that looked appealing to him. He had a strong sense of call to serve a small church in a poor community, but the available positions were at large suburban churches. So his first job out of seminary was in Canton, OH, doing community organizing for an ecumenical group of downtown churches. The work involved building bridges between churches and neighborhood housing and jobs programs. This allowed him to continue exploring the work of social justice, but it was not answering his deeper call to ministry. So he kept his eye open for small churches in low-income areas of Arizona, and in 1969, came across a little church in the Tucson area.

Southside Presbyterian Church was struggling to survive, though it had a rich history of cultural diversity and activism. Built in 1906 as a Presbyterian mission project, Southside was originally located in a Native American village just outside Tucson. By the end of World War II, the neighborhood included not only Tohono O'odham, but an increasing number of Mexican-Americans. After Southside called Mexican-American pastor Peter Samano, the makeup of the congregation increasingly matched the community. In 1956, Southside called a progressive African American pastor, who became president of Tucson's chapter of the NAACP and helped Southside play a vital role in desegregating some of Tucson's public facilities. But following Casper Glenn's departure in 1962, the church endured years of decline, and by 1969, there were only some twenty-five active members. The local governing body of the Presbyterian church was making plans to close Southside's doors.

For Fife, serving this struggling little church sounded like a dream job. Not only was it a cross-cultural church in an economically marginalized community, but many of its members were Tohono O'odham—the very people he had come to love during his summer internship. John made calls as to how he might apply for the job, but was told he was too late; the doors of Southside were set to be closed. He quickly arranged a meeting with church elders and told them he would love to serve as their pastor if they wanted to continue as a church. Southside's board worked with John to craft a proposal and presented it to the local presbytery and to the denominational Board of National Missions. They requested funds to support Southside as an experiment in church renewal and received such funding for two years.

The call presented a number of challenges for Fife. To begin with, the church's manse had been broken into, trashed, and was occupied by homeless people. Marianne took a look at the hole in the roof and told John she was not bringing their two young children to live *there*. After much effort by John to convince her that the place could quickly be fixed up, Marianne relented, though the days to come would prove more than a little trying on their marriage. Meanwhile, John had to pull together a congregation that could not even find the twenty-five members they *did* have. The pews were uncomfortable old plywood seats bolted to the floor. John was inexperienced, didn't speak Spanish, and didn't know the *barrio*.

Then there was the issue of music. At his first worship service, two elderly women played traditional hymns at a painfully slow tempo. John had seen music play a crucial role in the civil rights movement and in the worship life of local churches, and knew something had to be done if Southside was to have a future. John visited a service at neighboring Friendship Baptist Church and heard wonderful black gospel music performed with a full choir, directed by Rosie Johnson. The following Monday John was in Rosie's living room, tearfully begging her to help Southside with its music. She replied that she already had a job, but John countered that the Baptist service did not start until 11 a.m., and Southside could move its worship time up to 9:30 a.m. She could play at both services, he argued, and Rosie reluctantly agreed to give it a try. She would serve as Southside's music director for the next twenty-three years and prove crucial to its revitalization.

John's next step was to tear out the theater seats. Then he and the elders ventured out to visit present and former church members, telling them Southside was being resurrected. Having worked his way through college and seminary as a steel mill worker and a welder, John offered to dive into odd jobs at parishioners' homes. In so doing, he got to know their stories and to better understand the local community. Under John's leadership, Southside began to get involved again in local issues. They joined with some young Chicano organizers to stop plans to build a golf course in the *barrio*, arguing that a community center should be constructed instead. When he learned of murders taking place in the local prison, John helped organize street masses with the families of the deceased, raising awareness that helped to bring about prison reform. Church folk participated in campaigns for local land and water rights, and advocacy for improving medical care and education. By 1973, Southside had doubled its membership and was no longer facing questions about its viability!

John joined the Tucson Ecumenical Council, a coalition of sixty-five Catholic and Protestant churches that worked together on projects such as relocating Chilean refugees to the Tucson area. In 1980, John and the council became aware of an alarming international development. Through a reporting network of church workers serving in Guatemala and El Salvador, they learned that the bloodshed in Central America was far greater than American officials and the media were admitting. Salvadorans and Guatemalans who were fleeing the wars were arriving in Tucson with horrible stories, and some had marks of torture still evident on their flesh. The Immigration and Naturalization Service (INS) was picking these political refugees up and automatically sending them back to their countries, where they faced certain imprisonment or death. So the council formed a special task force on Central America to consider how to respond.

The task force began organizing volunteers to help jailed Central Americans held at the El Centro detention center. Bail was posted and asylum forms processed for those facing imminent deportation. In the course of this work, task force members learned a disturbing reality. Salvadoran and

Guatemalan refugees fleeing the violence in their countries had never learned they could apply for asylum in the United States, and if they *did* apply, asylum was being repeatedly denied. It was clear that the U.S. government did not want to acknowledge the state-sponsored violence that was driving Central Americans to flee, because it was supporting these repressive governments under the rubric of combating communism.

In 1981, John awoke in the middle of the night, going over in his mind a conversation he had just had with a local rancher named Jim Corbett, who shared his concern that U.S. immigration policy was refusing to acknowledge the refugee status of those fleeing. Jim told John that he and some other Quakers were going to pick up Central American refugees at the border and help them get across to the United States. "God bless you, Jim," John had said, congratulating him on his courage. But John felt his own agenda needed to be the legal defense project at the detention center, funded in part by the Presbyterian church, which had successfully tied up deportation processes. But in a quiet and determined fashioned, the squat rancher had laid out to the long-legged preacher a clear and convincing argument that if the U.S. government was actively rejecting refugees' rights to political asylum, active resistance to that unjust policy was the only ethical response. John was losing sleep as he ran over Jim's argument in his mind, finding it impossible to refute with a clear conscience. He called Corbett at 2 a.m. "All right, damn it, you're right. I'm in!"

A few days later, Jim called to say he had a family ready to cross in the morning. "I'll need you to pick them up at the border, and bring them to Tucson."

Crossing the Line: Sanctuary Activism

As John drove an hour and a half to the border, he wondered what he had gotten himself into. If he were caught by the Border Patrol, he would have his vehicle confiscated and end up spending the next couple of years in jail. This was a pivotal step he was taking, and he worried where it would take him next. This inaugural pick up went off without complication, but during future trips to pick up refugees at the border, John and Jim would often stop together in Tubac, a small town just north of Nogales. There the two would light a candle and pray, asking God for help in dealing with whatever that day might hold for them.

A consequence of John's border work was increased tension on the home front. "How can you risk two years in jail when you have two kids, our marriage, and your own future on the line?" Marianne would ask. John was grateful for the deep value Marianne placed on family. But he told her this work was not only vital to his ministry as a pastor, but touched on who he was as a human being, and to all that he believed. These tensions did not decrease when Southside began housing refugees on church grounds. Corbett had been taking in as many as twenty undocumented refugees at a time into his little one-bathroom adobe home and had appealed to John to see if Southside could help. After John brought the question before the church board, with much deliberation and a personal appeal from Jim, they voted in favor of opening Southside's doors. Southside thus became a "sanctuary" for refugees, providing temporary housing before escorting them to other faith communities within a loose but growing national network of safe havens.

Southside Church soon got word that the INS knew what they were doing and were warned to cease such efforts or risk indictment by the government. The Tucson Ecumenical Council task force held an emergency meeting in John's living room. All agreed they would continue to house refugees but now recognized that indictments would likely be a consequence. John suggested the idea of beating the government to the punch. Why not declare publicly that Southside Church and other willing churches, too, were "sanctuaries" for Central American refugees? That way they could frame and interpret what they were doing before arrests and publicity, thus making it clear that they were acting to save lives in a long-standing religious tradition. They could highlight the unjust immigration laws that denied asylum to those who pursued it legally and deported refugees back to the very state-sponsored violence from which they had fled. And they could make the case publicly that sheltering refugees was justified by international law, not to mention God's command to "do justice and love mercy" (Mi 6:8). This was an issue of both faith and conscience.

The council jumped on the idea, and John brought it to his congregation for a vote, which approved the initiative. The days leading up to the public announcement were the most tense of John's life. Marianne feared the possibility of prison time for her husband, while he worried a Sanctuary supporter might get arrested by the INS or the Border Patrol before the press conference. And it was proving a formidable challenge to find other churches similarly willing to declare Sanctuary. But on the eve of the declaration, four others churches stretching from Los Angeles to New York had signed on. So, on March 24, 1982—the second anniversary of Archbishop Oscar Romero's assassination in El Salvador—sitting at a table in front of his little Tucson church before forty reporters, Fife declared Southside Church a Sanctuary congregation. He introduced an undocumented refugee from El Salvador whom he called "Alfredo," and the man's bandana-covered face would soon become a symbol of the Sanctuary Movement. John declared that there were some one hundred churches around the nation supporting this "Central American Refugee Underground Railroad," invoking the name of the nineteenth-century network that had transported fugitive slaves from southern states to the North. In that spirit, Fife explained, the Sanctuary network was transporting refugees from one safe home to the next in order to avoid arrest and deportation by the INS. Individuals who were at the highest risk of being tortured or killed upon their return might be taken all the way to Canada. Southside Church announced itself as a sanctuary. John then sent the public declaration to the U.S. attorney general.

That evening, nearly a dozen clergy led more than two hundred people in a public march, followed by an interfaith worship service at Southside Church. They invited all faith-based communities to demonstrate solidarity with undocumented refugees. John insists today that they had no plans to start a broad social movement; the council was simply acting defensively, hoping to interpret their actions to the public before they were indicted and labeled "lawbreakers" by the government. Nevertheless, soon churches and organizations across the country began contacting John and the council, asking them about the movement and how to become a part of it. A growing number of faith communities declared themselves Sanctuary congregations, and media attention grew. The small Tucson volunteer force was quickly overwhelmed.

When John received a call from the Chicago Religious Task Force (CRTF) on Central America asking if he would be willing to lead a seminar for them on Sanctuary, he told them he was "up to his eyeballs" in work and couldn't possibly leave Tucson. A few days later, a task force member called back and said, "We've been talking, and it sounds like you all need some help. Can we do some resourcing for you on this whole Sanctuary idea?" John accepted their help with immense relief, and the CRTF began sending out educational material on Sanctuary. This material named Fife and Corbett as the movement's cofounders, which journalists picked up. In reality, however, Sanctuary was inaugurated through the decisions of various churches and synagogues, each of which had their own leadership and strategies. This decentralized, grassroots nature would prove one of its great strengths, and the movement's lack of organizational hierarchy meant it could continue even after John and other key players were tied up in court.

John describes Sanctuary as a self-selecting process that led the best and brightest to show up when they were most needed. For example, Katherine Flaherty, a former Peace Corps worker in El Salvador from 1977 to 1979, just showed up unannounced one evening at John and Marianne's house while they were having dinner. Though she didn't know a soul in Tucson, she said she was there to help and was given the job of running the Tucson Sanctuary office for the next four years. Another day, a twenty-year-old man from Philadelphia arrived in Tucson saying his home church was supporting him financially to serve as a "volunteer in mission" with Sanctuary. He was assigned to work with border crossings, and with what he learned, he later served as a delegate to negotiate with the United Nations on Guatemalan refugee visas (Crittenden 1988, 125).

As the movement grew, the media paid closer attention. In 1982, the television show *60 Minutes* featured the Sanctuary Movement, and in 1983 *Frontline* ran a similar feature. Both programs presented the U.S. government as insensitive to the struggle of Central American refugees, a media victory for Sanctuary supporters, and portrayed Corbett, Fife, and the movement in a positive light, infuriating the INS. Sanctuary actions were rightly framed in terms of "civil disobedience," nonviolently challenging unjust laws in the tradition of Gandhi and King. Corbett, however, preferred the phrase "civil initiative," which he understood from the legacy of the Nuremberg trials. If the international community could prosecute Nazis for failing to defy legalized murder under Hitler, Corbett reasoned, then there exists a standard higher than government laws to which citizens of any state are accountable. Still, in 1984 the government initiated an investigation, with wire taps and undercover agents posing as Sanctuary volunteers.

Meanwhile, tensions were growing between the CRTF and the Tucson Ecumenical Council's task force. Chicago felt that Sanctuary needed to be useful in furthering the revolutionary movement in Central America; consequently, they felt refugee victims of government repression should tell their stories in ways that would politicize people's perceptions. Tucson, on the other hand, felt that a commitment to human rights should transcend the politics of the Central American wars and emphasized the humanitarian nature of their intervention. While such differences initially seemed compatible, they would soon come to a head.

The turning point came one afternoon when John received a call from a rural health ministry north of Tucson. He was asked to pick up two fourteen-year-old Mayans who had fled when their mountain village was bombed by the Guatemalan army. The pair found a temporary home with farm workers in Marana, AZ; then John placed them on the Underground Railroad to a church out in Sumner, IL. Soon thereafter he received a message from the Chicago movement that the teens were too young and had no understanding of the conflict in Guatemala, so CRTF had sent them back to Marana because they were not appropriate Sanctuary spokespeople. Angry and troubled, John and Jim felt they had arrived at a clash of values with the CRTF.

These differences might have torn the Sanctuary Movement apart had not an event taken place that brought all the disparate players back together. In January 1985, a grand jury in Phoenix indicted John and fifteen other Sanctuary workers on charges of transporting, concealing, harboring, and shielding undocumented immigrants (see Cunningham 1995). This brought an unprecedented level of solidarity in the movement, as its various factions united to defend those indicted and address the heightened interest in Sanctuary from the media.

As the trial began, the judge ruled that absolutely no mention could be made of international law, or alleged persecution and violence suffered by the refugees, or anyone's religious convictions. This made it virtually impossible for the Sanctuary workers to defend themselves. The three deemed most likely to serve the minimum of eighteen months because of their active, visible, and vocal involvement in Sanctuary were Sr. Darlene Nicgorski, Philip Conger, and Fife. Prior to sentencing, John's attorney told him, "Take a toothbrush. The government went through this whole exercise to get some of you in prison."

Darlene was the first to be sentenced. The judge told her, "Sister, I'm going to be lenient in this case, and sentence you to five years probation on the condition that you have nothing more to do with this Sanctuary movement." Darlene replied, "Judge, you haven't been paying any attention at all. If you let me walk out of this courtroom on probation, I'm going to go right out and continue my Sanctuary work. So make up your mind what you want to do." John breathed a sigh of relief that he had not been first, doubting he would have made such a bold statement. The judge was not as impressed as John, grew red in the face, and called for an immediate recess. Fifteen minutes later he returned in exasperation to declare, "All right, five years probation, and you can take it up with your probation officer." Identical sentences were handed out for Fife and Conger. Though convicted as a felon for his Sanctuary work, John never did a single day of jail time.[1]

Churches continued to contact those working on the Underground Railroad to learn firsthand about Sanctuary. In response to such requests, an idea emerged to capitalize such interest to raise consciousness about issues on the border. If an official experiential education program were put in place, people could visit Tucson to see and hear about the plight of migrants and the injustice of U.S. immigration policy, and leave as potential agents of change. Recalling his own experience during the civil rights movement, John believed that you had to "be there on the ground" in order to understand the struggle. So in 1986, he tapped Rick Ufford-Chase to head up a new border education program.

In his early twenties, Ufford-Chase had just come off of an experiential education trip to Nicaragua with Witness for Peace and encountered liberation theology lived and practiced in a mountain village community. He was so moved that near the end of his trip he told one of the village elders, "God has called me to stay in Nicaragua and join you in your struggle." The elder replied that he had misunderstood the will of God and told Rick to go back to the United States and work for change there. Uncertain of the road ahead, Rick ran into a parish associate from Southside Church while traveling in Guatemala. She encouraged Rick to come to Tucson, and he soon joined the Sanctuary effort. Noticing Rick's leadership gifts and passion for justice, John figured he would be the perfect candidate to head up a new education initiative called "Borderlinks." Through visits, discussions, and lectures, visitors were invited to consider the realities of economic justice and immigration law. Borderlinks became an independent nonprofit organization in 1988.[2]

With the Tucson Ecumenical Council, John focused increasingly on leadership development, seeking out young people with organizing and leadership skills, a solid theology of liberation, and contagious passion for peace and justice. He encouraged such people to put down roots in Tucson, where he believed they would have strong community support in a long-term movement in a space where first and third worlds uniquely meet. Due largely to Sanctuary's efforts, the government agreed in 1989 to grant temporary protected status and work permits to refugees already living in the United States and to those who registered between 1989 and 1992. This brought a satisfying conclusion to the formal Sanctuary Movement but did not end John's efforts to build a thriving Tucson-based community of peace and justice activists committed for the long haul. He continued to be active in Presbyterian governing bodies, and in 1992 became moderator of the Presbyterian Church (U.S.A.)—the highest elected office in the denomination.

One of the Sanctuary Movement's great accomplishments, John believes, was allowing Central American refugees to share their stories of persecution with faith communities in North America. This helped convert many church people to a faith that pursues social as well as personal transformation and to realize they too could become "base communities," supporting one another in the vital but often arduous work of challenging injustice and oppression.

At the turn of the millennium, migrant deaths along the Arizona-Mexico border began skyrocketing in the wake of Operation Gatekeeper. This led Fife and other faith-rooted activists to found "Humane Borders," which provided and serviced water stations in the Sonoran desert near Tucson to save migrants from dehydration. Humane Borders distributed maps of the water stations and put up signs along high-trafficked areas to warn migrants *not* to make the dangerous desert crossing north. The organization also advocated allowing migrants legal access to medical aid, and de-criminalizing the provision of such aid. In July 2002, John joined others to found yet another organization, Samaritan Patrol (now called Tucson Samaritans/Los Samaritanos; see http://www.tucsonsamaritans.org). Taking its name from Jesus' parable about aiding a migrant who was attacked and left half-dead on the road (Lk 10:30–37), the Tucson Samaritans provide emergency food, water, and medical assistance to migrants in the desert. Those who volunteer on such patrols are greatly impacted by seeing the perils migrants encounter and hearing their stories of desperation, bravery, and survival.

By 2004, however, the number of men, women, and children who had died trying to cross the border since 1998 had reached 2000. So Fife, Ufford-Chase, and other faith-based activists met to form "No More Deaths," an umbrella organization that pulled together the various Tucson humanitarian and justice advocacy efforts on behalf of immigrants. The coalition included Borderlinks, the Catholic Diocese, migrant shelters, Coalicion de Derechos Humanos, and Frontera de Cristo. They felt that by coordinating these various efforts, they could have a more effective ministry and voice (see http://www.nomoredeaths.org). The organization strengthened existing efforts to provide food, water, and medical attention to migrants, monitored abuses in the borderlands, and brought the plight of migrants to national attention in order to change policies that had transformed the borderlands into a war zone.

In July 2005, Daniel Strauss and Shanti Sellz, two volunteers for No More Deaths, were arrested for taking three dying migrants to the hospital. Charged with two felonies and facing up to fifteen years in prison, the twenty-three-year-olds rejected a plea bargain that would have required them to admit guilt, arguing humanitarian aid was never a crime. Their charges were finally dismissed in 2007. In 2009, another volunteer with No More Deaths was found guilty of "littering" for leaving water containers in the Buenos Aires National Wildlife Refuge. Walt Staton said he would continue his work though he faced up to a year in prison for the charges. John saw young people from around the United States drawn to the work of Samaritans, Humane Borders, or No More Deaths, and enjoyed trying to convince them to become part of a long-term community of transformation in Tucson. He believes such leadership development is crucial to Tucson's tradition of providing aid and advocacy to the immigrants on its doorstep.

John retired after thirty-five years of pastoring Southside Presbyterian Church in 2005. He remains in Tucson, active with No More Deaths and Samaritans (see Goodman 2007). Some of his favorite activities now are falconry and spending time with his six grandchildren, which, he quips, "beats the hell out of working." But his long ministry of crossing the boundaries between the United States and Mexico, between insiders and outsiders, and between the vocations of "pastor" and "prophet" represents a compelling example of Jesus' gospel of inclusion without borders.

9

Gospel Nativities vs.
Anti-Immigrant Nativism

Ched Myers

*And he arose and took the Child and his
mother by night, and departed to Egypt. (Mt 2:14)*

The popular version of the Christmas story that is sung
in carols and portrayed in church manger scenes throughout North America has become so domesticated that it offers little antidote to the consumer frenzy of our holiday
celebrations. It is also a highly selective conflation of the
two gospel accounts of Jesus' birth, which in fact have few
details in common. Yet Matthew 1–2 and Luke 1–2 agree
on a basic theme that is almost entirely obscured by sentimentalized Christmas pageantry: that God slips quietly into
a world of brutal rulers and hard-pressed refugees, and that
only a few unheralded people manage to recognize the
presence and act conscientiously.

The biographical literature of Roman antiquity, much
like the "infotainment" media in our culture, focused almost exclusively upon rich and famous personalities as its
subjects. The gospels, in contrast, feature poor folk as the
true protagonists of history. The central characters in the

Christmas story are a rural peasant couple displaced by powerful political, economic, and military forces in Roman Palestine that they cannot understand. Maria and Jose are far from pious superheroes—indeed, the legitimacy of the child is in question (Mt 1:18f), and their low social status is indicated by their inability to procure lodging when in desperate straits (Lk 2:7). But they are spiritually powerful, sensitive to dreams (Mt 1:22–23, 2:15, 2:23) and visions (Lk 1:26ff).

The Holy Family is distinguished by the courage to endure harsh conditions (Maria gives birth in a barn; Lk 2:16) and to make hard choices (fleeing the country; Mt 1:14–15). Surrounding them, meanwhile, is a dubious and obscure cast of characters: elderly crones (Lk 1:5–25, 2:25–38), caring relatives (Lk 1:39ff), strange foreign emissaries (Mt 2:1f), animal herdsmen (Lk 2:8–20), and fellow refugees (Mt 2:16–18). Yet they are also accompanied by mysterious heavenly messengers, who offer startling interpretations of these obscure events at the margins of history, suggesting that somehow Maria's back-alley birthing will pose a sharp challenge to the dominating colonial rule of Caesar (Lk 2:9–14) and Herod (Mt 2:3–6).

These biblical nativity stories, in their focus on the improvisational struggle for life by people of conscience in the midst of overbearing imperial strategies of death, can serve as an alternative moral compass not only during the Christmas season, but for discerning what immigrant justice means today. To help us see the connections, I will read these stories in conversation with how they have been appropriated by Latino culture.

Baby Jesus, Refugee: Matthew's Story

Matthew's birth narrative is composed around three elements:

1. a genealogy (1:1–17);
2. Jose's dreams (1:18–25, 2:13–15, 2:19–23); and
3. the murderous plotting of King Herod (2:1–12, 2:16–18).

The latter two are woven together into five "scenes," which constitute the first "act" in the theater of the first gospel. Each scene turns on a citation from the Hebrew Bible:

1. Matthew 1:18–25: Jesus' birth, Jose's first dream (1:23; Is 7:14);
2. Matthew 2:1–12: Herod, Child and Magi, Jose's second dream (2:6; Mi 5:2);
3. Matthew 2:13–15: The Holy Family's flight (2:15; Hos 11:1);
4. Matthew 2:16–18: Herod's reaction (2:17f; Jer 31:15); and
5. Matthew 2:19–23: Return to Nazareth, Jose's third dream (2:23; Is 11:1).

By relating the events surrounding Jesus' birth to the prophetic tradition, the evangelist seeks to strengthen credibility and anchor the events in the wider scope of salvation history. The three dream sequences are a literary vehicle with much the same function and are identical in structure. Each time a deteriorating plot is interrupted by an angel who appears to Jose (Mt 1:20, 2:13, 2:19). The angel issues a command, along with its rationale; Jose then "gets up" and obeys (1:24f, 2:14f, 2:21). These revelations signal that YHWH is intimately involved on the side of the weak and disenfranchised in a struggle with the powers (represented by Herod) for true sovereignty.

It is easy to skip over those boring "begats" that form the prologue to Matthew's Nativity story, but this "family tree" has a few surprises—and a lot to say about how God works in history. In traditional societies, persons derive their identity from their clan, in stark contrast to the individualism of modern culture. Matthew's ancestral roll call would have been the normal and expected way to introduce and commend Jesus to his Jewish audience. The genealogy comes in three parts (see 1:17), invoking each major epoch in the saga of Israel: the patriarchal era (Abraham et al. 1:1–6), the monarchy (David et al. 1:6–11), and the exile and restoration (Mt 1:12–16).

But it is the way in which Matthew *departs* from a strictly patriarchal family line that captures our attention. Five women, inclusive of Mary, appear in the list; even more disturbing to tradition is the fact that these are women of "dubious" character. Tamar (1:13) posed as a prostitute in order to compel Judah into fulfilling his obligations according to the customs of Levirate marriage (Gn 38). Rahab (Mt 1:5) ran a Canaanite brothel but saved Joshua and his spies by hiding them and then lying to royal security forces in Jericho (Jo 2). Ruth (Mt 1:5) was a Moabite who seduced Boaz to gain entry to his clan (Ru 3). And the "wife of Uriah" (Bathsheeba; Mt 1:6) was the object of King David's infamous adultery and murderous cover-up (2 Sm 11). It appears that Matthew intentionally associates Maria, the peasant-girl mother of Jesus (Mt 1:16), with other women of "unusual" sexual circumstances—and the first scene of the drama explains why.

In first-century Jewish culture, marriage was arranged between families. A "contract of consent" was drawn up when the girl was about thirteen; she then continued to live at home for up to a year, until she was "transferred" to her husband's house and support. It is during this time of "betrothal" that Mary is found to be pregnant (1:18). Because Torah required that adultery be punished with stoning (Dt 22:20f), Jose refuses to make this a public issue and plans instead to divorce without pressing charges (Mt 1:19). At this point he has his first dream, in which he is instructed not only to go forward with the transfer of Maria to his house, but to become the legal father of the child. To name Jesus publicly functions as an acknowledgement of paternity—effectively "covering" for the Holy Spirit! And Isaiah's royal moniker, "Emmanuel," puts this act firmly in a political context (1:23; Is 7:14).

In light of the implied village scandal, Matthew's twists to the genealogy suggest that he does not necessarily assume the credulity of his audience. While believers may affirm the virgin birth of Jesus, Matthew recognizes that the *appearance* of Jesus' illegitimacy remains. He, too, is "covering" for the Spirit, placing Maria in an extraordinary line of women who, despite (or perhaps because of) questionable circumstances, have played key roles in liberation history. Indeed, the next episode will allude back to the extraordinary conspiracy of women who rescued the prophet Moses from an imperial pogrom (Ex 1). This reminds us of a central truth of incarnational theology: God's redemptive purpose works in and through real human situations, in all their ambiguity—*especially* through courageous women willing to defy oppressive social conventions in order to embrace the alternative vision of God.

Matthew 2 turns to the story of Herod and the Holy Family, a narrative full of violence and risk. Matthew's account presents an archetypal portrait of a paranoid tyrant, a description that could well fit either Herod the Great (who died either in 4 or 1 BCE) or his successor sons who ruled in the region of the story: Archelaus (ethnarch of Samaria, Judea, and Edom from 4 BCE to 6 CE) and Antipas (tetrarch of Galilee and Perea from 4 BCE to 39 CE). Richard Horsley writes: "Quite apart from any particular incident that may underlie it, the story portrays a network of historical relationships that prevailed in the general circumstance of the birth of the messiah" (1989, 40). He details how the Herodians served Rome's interests in colonial Palestine, oppressing their own people with taxes to fund grandiose building projects, and "instituted what today would be called a police-state, complete with loyalty oaths, surveillance, informers, secret police, imprisonment, torture and brutal retaliation against any serious dissenter" (46f). Horsley concludes: "Matthew 2 comes to life vividly against the background of Herodian exploitation and tyranny" (49).

Matthew's narrative is also inspired, however, by two stories from the Hebrew Bible, which add deeper layers of political critique. The first allusion is to Numbers 22–23, in which the Canaanite king Balak summons the prophet Balaam "from the east" (Nm 23:7) to curse Israel (22:6), only to be betrayed when Balaam instead pronounces blessing (23:8ff). In Matthew, Herod is double-crossed by Magi "from the east," whom he had employed to locate Jesus the child-king (ostensibly to "bless" him; Mt 2:1ff). At issue here is political legitimacy. The astrologers seek a star, a cosmic symbol in antiquity signaling the birth of a great leader. Herod, the client despot, is understandably disturbed that these foreigners have named the child "King of the Jews" (2:1–2)—Herod's own title! The incipient challenge to his hegemony is deepened when Herod's assembled advisers remind him of the prophetic oracle promising that a Messianic ruler will come from "one of the little clans of Judah" (2:4–6; Mi 5:2).

As is the way of the powerful (then and now), Herod cloaks his sinister "counterinsurgency" plan in pious pretense: he wishes to "pay homage" to the Child (Mt 2:8). The astrologers, however, are not fooled. Finding Jesus, they offer him gifts befitting true political authority, thereby rendering their allegiance, then turn heel and slip out of the country. Horsley provides fascinating historical context for the *magoi,* who were "originally a caste of highest ranking politico-religious advisers or officers of the Median emperor, then in the Persian imperial court" (1989, 53). These sages and seers wielded legendary political influence, which explains why in earliest Christian tradition they were portrayed both as "wise men" and "kings." More importantly, *magoi* may well "have been instrumental in opposing the Hellenistic imperial forces that conquered them and other ancient Near Easter peoples. . . . Throughout the first century CE, there was a continuing confrontation if not outright war between the Romans and the Parthian empire to the East. It is not difficult to imagine that the Magi would have been associated with the eastern empire in opposition to Rome" (55f). Their actions in Matthew are, therefore, both conscientious *and* politically subversive.

For a second time, Jose receives instructions in a dream (Mt 2:13). Matthew shapes the character of Jesus' father after the great patriarch Joseph, who was called "the dreamer" and went away to Egypt (Gn 37)—which is precisely where the Holy Family flees to escape Herod's wrath (Mt 2:14). So does the savior of the world begin life as a political refugee.

These actions of holy obedience are at the same time risky acts of political *dis*obedience, and call to mind a second story from the Hebrew Bible. Exodus 1–2 narrates the birth of Moses, whose life is similarly threatened by a paranoid potentate, and also saved by an "underground railroad." The parallels between Pharaoh and Herod are uncanny: the challenge of an infant unleashes a policy of infanticide —justified by "national security" (Ex 1:16–20). Royal attempts to work through accomplices (Pharaoh's midwives, Herod's astrologers) fail, however, because these characters choose life and are prepared to deceive their superiors in order to protect the innocent. We never again hear of these role players—yet upon their acts of costly conscience hangs the whole of the biblical drama. Dare we assume that our own choices, minor characters though we also be, are any less consequential? And does not Matthew's story cast a new light on experiments in faith and immigrant justice such as the New Sanctuary Movement (see Chapter 3)?

As we shall see in the next section, the gospel nativity stories are deeply significant to the culture of Mexican America, in large part because they speak so poignantly to Latino realities. For example, midway through the Advent season, the Feast of *La Virgen de Guadalupe* is celebrated (December 12). Guadalupe is the patroness of indigenous peasants displaced by Spanish colonization, who clearly identified herself with the "abandoned" ones. Her image in Catholic iconography represents an extraordinary, eclectic affirmation of both Catholic and Aztec religious symbolism (see Elizondo 2002) and is important to Latinos throughout the U.S. Southwest (it was carried by farmworker organizer Cesar Chavez in all his marches).

But Guadalupe is portrayed in a fashion that, for the biblically literate, is also germane to Matthew's Nativity story. Her famous image is based on the apocalyptic "portent" seen by John the Revelator in the middle of his evocative visionary cycles:

> A great portent appeared in heaven: a woman clothed with the sun, with the moon under her feet, and on her head a crown of twelve stars. She was pregnant and was crying out in birth pangs, in the agony of giving birth. Then another portent appeared in heaven: a great red dragon. . . . Then the dragon stood before the woman who was about to bear a child, so that he might devour her child as soon as it was born. And she gave birth to a son. (Rv 12:1–5)

The dragon is a master symbol used by John, a political prisoner in the late first century CE, to represent the lethal violence of the Roman Empire. The dragon's intent to "devour the child" is a clear allusion to both Matthew's gospel tale of Herod and the old Exodus story of Pharaoh. Like the mother of Moses and Maria of Nazareth, Revelation's "woman clothed with the sun" gives birth to a child in the teeth of the Beast, nurturing life in defiance of the power of death. Guadalupe stands for, and with, all those who do the same under the shadow of a different empire today.

In Matthew's narrative the empire inevitably strikes back, and the slaughter of innocents ensues (Mt 2:16ff). The Bible is so much clearer than we are about the violent realities of Statecraft! "Rachel weeps" (Mt 2:17f; Jer 31:14) over such an absurd mismatch: kings vs. kids! Yet such is the paradox of biblical history. As imperial minds plot genocide, God's messengers enter the world at risk: floating down the Nile in a reed basket (Ex 2:3), spirited out of the country on back roads (Mt 2:14). Against the presence of power is pitted the power of presence: God with us.

This terrible tale is commemorated in the Feast of the Holy Innocents on December 28. Not well-known by North American Christians, it was instituted by the Latin Church in the fifth century, perhaps anticipating that the Nativity season would become too sentimentalized, too innocuous, and too triumphal in a comfortable Christendom (how right it was!). So this feast was wisely instituted to preserve the "underside" of the Christmas story, a sharp counterpoint to pious pageantry.

The Feast of the Holy Innocents offers a grim reminder that there was and is a political cost to the incarnation—that Jesus was born not in a palace but in a feed trough to parents who were refugees, not royalty. The Bible is clear from beginning to end that the principalities and powers—represented by corporate managers and political operatives and military strategists in every age—are forever threatened by the God who invades our world from below. In the name of national security, suspects (and all others who fit the profile) must be contained and neutralized, undocumented people criminalized as potential "terrorist threats." The result: "A voice is heard in Ramah"—the sound of women mourning their children.

The somber feast interrupts our year-end reveling with the discomforting thought that behind the obfuscating rhetoric of "regime change" or "sealing our borders" is the terrible reality of human lives caught in the crossfire or expiring in the desert. It is disproportionately women and children on the business end of our security sweeps, surgical strikes, and deportation campaigns. Perhaps this is why the Feast of the Holy Innocents is routinely ignored by our churches as an inconvenient intrusion of both Word and World on our insular holiday feasting. But because infants continue to be victimized by emperors, it is a painful and importunate gift to have a feast day that invites us to—no, demands that we—remember the suffering of innocents that continues from the horn of Africa to the Amazon, and from Gaza to the U.S.-Mexico border. Coming just before our year-in-review rituals and our New Year's resolution making, it challenges us to include in our purview the lives of those who are at risk. The Christ child bids us live with eyes wide open to a world full of disappeared, homeless, trafficked, and traumatized children, so many of whom are immigrants.

Matthew's Nativity tale concludes with Jose's third and final dream (2:19–23). Herod's death allows a return to Palestine, but the danger remains, and the Holy Family settles in an obscure frontier village. It is there at the margins that Jesus grows up, until the day he will commence his public mission to face down the powers once and for all.

This Christmas story is a much-needed, if painful, corrective to the holiday season's saccharine spirituality and cacophonous commercialism. Matthew speaks frankly about political violence, displacement, and danger—which is to say, of real life as it is for the poor. Here is a story for *our* world, which still teems with refugees, lamenting mothers, and the duplicitous schemes of the powerful. But *this* is the world in which God is with us, into which God has come and yet will come. The only question is, will *we* recognize the presence and act accordingly?

Posadas sin Fronteras: Luke's Story

It is a few nights before Christmas 1994. A small group of us are singing timidly, clutching candles against a chilly drizzle. We slowly make our way up a muddy hill. Below us an orange glow floats like fog above the border checkpoint at San Ysidro, CA. "*En nombre del cielo, les pido posada,*" sings an unseen group on the Tijuana side of the border fence. "*Pues no puede andar mi esposa amada*" ("In the name of Heaven I beg you for lodging, for my beloved wife cannot walk"). Between us is a menacing ten-foot high metal wall, donated to the U.S. Border Patrol by the Pentagon after Desert Storm—one war's surplus bolstering another war's front lines. We respond: "*Aquí no es mesón; sigan adelante. Yo no puedo abrir; no sea algun tunante*" ("This is not an inn, so keep going. I cannot open, for you may be bad people").

We are celebrating the first "*Posada sin Fronteras.*" The idea came from the late Roberto Martinez, a colleague in the American Friends Service Committee who worked tirelessly on immigrant human rights in and around San Diego. Roberto introduced me to the tough landscape of these borderlands, from the sweaty *maquiladoras* to the canyons where farmworkers live in caves and plastic tents in the shadow of affluent trophy homes. He became legendary for his documentation of hundreds of Border Patrol abuses each year, ranging from verbal abuse, illegal confiscation of documents, and deportation of legal residents to maimings, rapes, and deaths in pursuit or in custody (see Chapter 10).

Always looking for fresh ways to communicate the stories he saw daily, Roberto suggested that perhaps a *Posada* could be held at the border fence to recontextualize the bitter drama of immigrant homelessness. The old Catholic tradition of *Las Posadas* ("lodging, shelter") is celebrated each Advent throughout the Southwest to commemorate Luke's story of Maria and Jose's difficult journey from Nazareth to Bethlehem in search of shelter. A procession through the *barrio* is usually led by a child dressed as an angel, followed by musicians and people carrying figures of Maria and Jose. At an appointed house, the group divides in two, and a poignant litany is recited or sung at the threshold; then the doors are opened and a *fiesta* ensues.

Roberto's idea became the seed of the "*Posada sin Fronteras*," reimagined by church and immigrant rights activists from Tijuana and San Diego. Groups gather on both sides of the wall, watched carefully by the Border Patrol and, more recently, by anti-immigrant counterprotestors. The U.S. side recites the role of the innkeeper in the litany, the Mexican side that of the Holy Family—and the story comes uncomfortably alive right at the heart of the border war zone. This powerful public liturgy has continued each year since that inaugural experiment in 1994.

We hold aloft three large piñatas representing Maria, Jose, and the innkeeper. For as far as we can see, the no-man's-land of the border is bathed by floodlights, and thick with U.S. Border Patrol vehicles and helicopters. These "innkeepers" spend millions of taxpayer dollars in an effort to reduce illegal entries across this, the world's most heavily used border crossing, one of the only places on earth where first and third world lay side by side. Their mission is to keep out the very ones who, more than a century earlier, were expressly invited *into* the United States in the extraordinary verse of the immigrant poet Emma Lazarus inscribed on the Statue of Liberty.

> Give me your tired, your poor,
> Your huddled masses yearning to breathe free,
> The wretched refuse of your teeming shore.
> Send these, the homeless, tempest-tost to me,
> I lift my lamp beside the golden door.

But what immigrants and economic refugees see first today at this new portal is not the hospitable face of a woman holding aloft that lamp, but rather the stern face of heavily armed Border guards, intent on apprehending, incarcerating, and deporting the "homeless and tempest-tossed." So at this conflicted, contested, and increasingly militarized door, activists gather to reenact the old, sacred story about how God struggles to enter a world of hard-hearted inhospitality.

The refrain of Jose resounds from across the wall: "*No seas inhumano; ténnos caridad. Que el Dios de los cielos te lo pagará*" ("Don't be inhuman; have mercy on us. The God of the heavens will reward you for it."). We sing the traditional *Posadas* litany back and forth across the wall hearing but not seeing one another. To symbolize our solidarity, green ribbons are passed through small holes in the fence. "We pray that the day will come when we can have this *Posada* truly without borders," says a local Bishop to the crowd. "If we reject the poor, we are rejecting Jesus Christ himself." Turning up the collar of my coat against the cold, I marvel at this liturgy of resistance to this wall that runs right through the heart of this congregation—and of our church and nation. It is precisely this nontraditional geography that brings this old pageantry painfully alive again.

"Ya se pueden ir, y no molestar," threatens the innkeeper's verse. *"Porque si me enojo les voy a pegar"* ("Better go on, and don't bother us. For if I become angry, I shall beat you up."). Behind us a knot of Border Patrol officers keep a watchful eye, as an activist colleague next to me laments about the trend of increased Border Patrol abuses. When the liturgy finishes, doves are released and fly off, unrestrained by the metal fence, a small sign of hope amidst this free fire zone in the war against the poor, the New Global Economic Order's Berlin Wall.

Las Posadas remembers Luke's story of a poor couple, pregnant with a prophet, who became homeless because of the push and pull of imperial forces. At its heart is the litany, a conversation that putatively takes place through a closed door. It is a tense, dramatic exchange between insiders and outsiders. The door represents the ultimate liminal space, the threshold between home and homelessness (see Chapter 3 above). At the border fence it becomes a sort of community theater in real political space that takes on an almost unbearable poignancy, bearing witness to immigrant suffering. And the more we know about the social and literary character of Luke's nativity, the more relevant and subversive this theater becomes.

Luke's birth narrative opens and closes with Temple vignettes about elderly couples who are waiting patiently for God's intervention in their tired history: Zechariah and Elizabeth (Lk 1:5–25) and Simeon and Anna (2:25–38). But Luke has a gendered "edge": at the outset a male priest is silenced (1:5–23), while two women pregnant with prophets take center stage, encouraging one another and embodying faith (1:24–45). And the last word in Luke's Christmas story also belongs to a woman, the prophet Anna (2:36–38).

The long tradition of singing carols during Christmas is rooted in Luke's account, which is composed around three canticles: Mary's "Magnificat" (1:46–55), Zechariah's "Benedictus" (1:68–79), and Simeon's "Nunc Dimittis" (2:29–32). These traditional titles (derived from the opening words of each song in Latin) should not obscure the fact that each is a fierce chant of nationalist hope by oppressed Jews into the teeth of the violent Roman occupation of Palestine. The Magnificat (based upon the ancient "Song of Hannah"; 1 Sm 2:1–10), is a stirring revolutionary hymn that envisions YHWH's liberation of Israel and a radical social and political leveling (Lk1:51–55)! And when Zechariah (Lk 1:79) and Simeon (2:29) sing of "peace," it is *not* referring to the "Pax Romana" but the subversive peace mission of a marginalized Messiah.

Of all the evangelists, Luke gives the most detail about the political context of the Jesus story. The events occur during the reign of "Caesar Augustus" and "Quirinius the governor of Syria" (2:1f), and later the rule of Tiberius, Pilate, and Herod (3:1f). Luke wants his reader to be clear that *this* story is taking place in real political time and space— something often lost on modern North American readers, who imagine the gospel as a cosmic drama with no real terrestrial tether. But as soon as Luke has named the imperial officials who *think* they are in charge of history, he immediately swings his focus on to the poor people who will *change* history: the obscure Jose (2:4), and the fiery wilderness prophet John the Baptist (3:2).

The Holy Family is pulled from their home by the empire's demand for a census (2:1). Residents of Palestine were compelled to travel to the village of their ancestors to be counted so that they could better be "managed" by the Roman military government (2:3f). In Luke's account of Jose's unwilling journey from Nazareth to Bethlehem, there is an obvious implication typically ignored by interpreters. The fact that he is denied lodging in Bethlehem can mean only one thing: every one of Jose's kin had *also* been displaced from their hometown by the political and economic forces of empire. This is how Maria ends up giving birth to Jesus in a feed trough, accompanied by animals and their herders (2:7). (Such displacement continues for Palestinians in Bethlehem today, a town that is divided and locked down by an Israeli security wall even more formidable than the one at the U.S.-Mexico border.)

The birth of a "Savior and Lord" (2:11) is accompanied by the angelic host singing "Glory to God in the highest and on earth peace" (2:14). Though these phrases are mere Christmas card greetings today, they were originally highly political, applied exclusively to Caesar Augustus. Moreover, this "good news" is entrusted not to political and religious leaders, but to a group of anonymous shepherds—a class of workers considered "unclean" and unreliable by polite society of the time (2:8, 15–20). Just as Matthew's story opposes Jesus' "rule" to Herod's, so Luke heralds a political challenge to Rome. No wonder Luke includes a "reality check": this new vision will be opposed by many, and will have a cost (2:34–35).

After the "epilogue" to Luke's nativity tale (2:41–52), Jose disappears from the story—whether it is an early death by poverty or jailing by the military we are not told—so that Jesus is brought up in a single parent home (see 4:22). It is little wonder then that Jesus would emphasize in his later teaching the very thing he was denied at birth: hospitality, which he insists should be extended to *all* people, even one's enemies (see 7:1–9, 23:42f)!

The scenario we enact in a *Posada* tells us a lot about the struggle of poor folk across the ages to survive the social disruption wrought by empire. It certainly resonates with the experiences of those who tell their stories each year at the *Posada sin Fronteras*, who have been pulled from villages in Oaxaca or Zacatecas, Chalatenango or Morazan, Jalapa or Coban. They testify to long, arduous journeys that have brought them to the Mexican side of the border fence, only to face the most dangerous crossing. And if that is successful, an uncertain future awaits them in a country increasingly hostile to their presence—even as it is increasingly dependent upon their low wage labor.

The traditional *Posadas* litany has a happy ending: in the ritual, the innkeeper finally recognizes the Holy Family, and intones, "Enter, holy pilgrims, receive this corner, for though this dwelling is poor, I offer it with all my heart." "Blessed is the house that today offers protection," comes Jose's response, "blessed is this house that gives us shelter." This is not, of course, what happens at the border *Posada*. Instead, the door remains closed; all participants can do as they shower each other with sweets thrown over the wall, is to make solemn commitments to bring that wall down—and just as importantly, to refuse to let it be internalized in our hearts.

A few years ago we celebrated *Las Posadas* on the border just days after federal agents had raided meat-processing plants in six states. In a new wrinkle in the war on immigrants, Immigration and Customs Enforcement agents charged undocumented workers with "identity-theft," in order to exonerate the company and scapegoat the workers. To criminalize undocumented immigrants—already the most vulnerable among us from both an economic and human rights perspective—is to willfully obscure not only the deeper and wider issues of justice, but also the root cause. The push and pull of empire that displaced the Holy Family still forces people to leave their homes in order to survive. Identity theft? It is we who have lost our identity as immigrant peoples and as Christians who follow a refugee Messiah. Yet the spirit of *Las Posadas* remains alive, for some local people in the Midwest opened their homes to the children of workers taken into custody in those raids, and a few police even refused to cooperate with the sweeps. In those moments, the gospel of Nativity trumped the ideology of nativism!

The *Posadas sin Fronteras* public liturgy is now spreading to different sites along the border. The simple act of relocating worship into contested political space recovers the Nativity as a *real-world* saga. It rescues Christmas from its trivialization by spiritualizing pietism and relentless commercialism, while compelling us to confront the hardships so familiar to those forced to become "sojourners" in order to support their families. For those of us who are privileged in a world of violence and exclusion, hearing the pleas of the "Josés" on the other side of the border fence, and having to take on the role of the hard-hearted *casero* (innkeeper) in the *Posadas* litany, is searing to heart and conscience. It animates us to rediscover what it means to raise the lamp of prophetic hospitality beside the no-longer-Golden American Door. This *is* the Christmas story, then and now, and we Christians need to get it right.

10

Defending Human Rights in the Borderlands: Roberto Martinez

Matthew Colwell

You shall not pervert the justice due an alien. (Dt 24:17)

On July 9, 2011, a memorial library was dedicated to Roberto Martinez at the Friends Center in San Diego. Two hundred people gathered to honor the legendary human rights work pioneered at the U.S.-Mexico border by Roberto, who died in 2009. Veteran local activists, such as David Valladolid, Jess Haro, and Enrique Morones, joined Roberto's widow Yolanda and American Friends Service Committee staff persons Christian Ramirez and Pedro Rios to honor his legacy. Each speaker noted that although Roberto had received wide recognition and numerous awards from both government officials and activist groups on both sides of the border, he remained a genuinely humble man who nevertheless sustained a fire in his belly for immigrant rights.

Call to Activism

A fifth-generation U.S. citizen and former farmworker, Roberto grew up knowing intimately how America was a "house divided," discriminating against brown-skinned people like him. This lesson was drummed into him at sixteen, when a Border Patrol agent tapped him on the shoulder. "*Sus papeles?*" the agent asked. Roberto was washing dishes in the kitchen at a small San Diego restaurant. Raised in a household that spoke only English, Roberto did not understand the request.

"What do you want?" Roberto responded.

Surprised to hear Roberto replying in English, the agent said, "Your identification papers, please."

"I'm a U.S. citizen," Roberto said.

"Can you prove it?"

"No, but here, look, I'm a student." He handed the agent his student identification card.

Unconvinced, the agent told him, "You'll have to come with me."

It was 1954, and "Operation Wetback" was in full swing, a national effort to crack down on illegal immigration. Those who looked to be of Latin American descent were routinely rounded up and sent to Mexico. Unaware of his rights at the time, Roberto figured he had little choice but to follow the agent. He was led to a back alley, where a van was waiting. Roberto took a seat in the back alongside others similarly apprehended and learned they were all about to be taken across the border. Roberto was terrified. He had no family, friends, or contacts in Tijuana, nor did he have any form of official identification to get back across to the United States.

When the van reached the border, the passengers were unloaded, and the agents prepared to escort them on foot across. Roberto protested, "I don't have any relatives in Mexico. I don't know anybody there. I don't have any money, and I'm only sixteen years old. What am I supposed to do?" A supervisor came and questioned Roberto for a few minutes, finally telling Roberto he was free to go. "Go where?" Roberto asked. "I'm fifteen miles from where I live and work."

"Call somebody!" The supervisor said curtly, and went back to join the other agents. Roberto phoned various family members without any luck, until he reached his grandfather, who came to pick him up. The episode was a rude awakening for Roberto to the injustice in the U.S. immigration system. In the weeks that followed, Roberto was stopped repeatedly on the street by police, often pushed around or picked up and brought downtown for questioning about persons and crimes with which he had no connection. Border Patrol agents accosted him, demanding that he prove his U.S. citizenship. Such harassment and injustice would be precisely what he would spend his adult life combating.

Years later, three mothers and their four high school-age children stood at the doorway of Roberto's home. As he glanced at the three boys and the one girl, he noted visible injuries on all four, especially the bright purple bruises on the girl's neck and side of her mouth. After inviting them in, Roberto asked what had happened. "We got beat up again," the young people said. "They waited for us after school with sticks and were yelling, 'Go back to Mexico, Wetbacks.' When the sheriffs came they only arrested us Mexican kids, and put us in juvenile hall." The girl's throat injuries, he was told, were from being choked by the sheriffs.

This was not the first time Roberto had heard of racist attacks outside San Diego's Santana High School. Since his own kids had begun attending there, Roberto heard how groups of white students would come to school with T-shirts reading "White Power" or "Youth Klan Core." At a supermarket parking lot across the street from the high school, some would verbally harass the darker-skinned students, attacking them at times with baseball bats and two-by-fours.

Though a quiet, unassuming young father and shy by nature, Roberto had recently begun to emerge within the local Mexican-American community as a soft-spoken but determined leader. He had founded and subsequently directed a Chicano community group at the local Catholic church. He suspected it was this leadership role that had led these folks to his door. Seeing the fear and pain in their eyes caused something within him to snap. "I'm going to do something about this," he said, picking up the phone. His first call was to Santana High School. "I want a meeting tomorrow morning, ten o'clock, to talk about this," he told the vice principal.

"It's already been resolved," was the reply. "The sheriffs have taken care of it."

"No," Roberto said, "they haven't," and put down the phone. He then called the sheriff. "I need a meeting tomorrow at ten o'clock," he repeated. "There are some police brutality problems here."

"It's all resolved" the sheriff retorted. "It's been taken care of." Frustrated, Roberto put down the phone and sat to consider his next move. He recalled the times he had suffered humiliation and abuse by police and Border Patrol, and thought of the fear and the pain he'd observed in the faces of his seven visitors. Next he prayed, asking God for guidance and direction. As a plan began to coalesce in his mind, his prayer became a request for assistance in the task ahead, asking for strength and courage to step boldly into unfamiliar waters of confronting injustice. Then he picked up the phone again.

Roberto reached the vice principal, and announced: "I want a meeting at the school tomorrow morning at 10:00 a.m. If you don't sit with us, I'm going to call the media and hold a press conference in front of the school. And we are going to call this what it is: *racial violence*, which you are approving and condoning. You are allowing this Youth Klan Corp to recruit!"

There was silence on the other end of the line for a moment. "OK, we'll meet."

Roberto then called the sheriff back. "Your deputies are exacerbating a very violent situation. I want you or one of your representatives at a meeting at Santana High School tomorrow at ten o'clock. If nobody from your office is there, I'm going to call the media and have a press conference in front of your station, and I'll declare publicly how the police are contributing to the racial violence at the high school by their actions. And we will also picket in front of your station." The sheriff said a lieutenant would be there.

The next morning more than a dozen concerned Mexican-American parents met with the vice principal and police lieutenant in the high school auditorium. After listening to the parents' concerns, the vice principal agreed not to let Klan Corp shirts be worn on school campus and promised the school would have someone monitoring the safety of students as they left each day. The lieutenant promised both to discipline the officers involved and to monitor the situation, ensuring students' protection. Roberto was on campus the following afternoon to make sure that both police and school representatives were monitoring things. With such oversight, the violence dissipated.

Roberto came away from the experience changed. He had seen firsthand what could be accomplished by organizing the community around a particular issue of injustice, and had observed how threats of protest and publicity could have a catalyzing impact. As word got out about what he had accomplished at Santana High School, Roberto began to get calls from Spring Valley, Lemon Grove, Oceanside, and Escondido complaining about harassment and violence by police and Border Patrol. In the days to come, he would learn how to file complaints, how to match families with attorneys in order to file formal lawsuits, and how to organize public protests. And he discovered a passion for justice work.

After his graduation from high school in 1955, Roberto spent most of the next twenty years working for Rohr industries, an aerospace manufacturing company in Chula Vista. Starting as an entry-level machine shop worker, he worked his way up the ladder, eventually becoming an engineer earning good money and supervising teams of more than thirty others. As his income and responsibilities grew, however, Roberto found his heart drawn to the activist projects in which he was engaged in his scant free time. In the wake of his success at Santana High School, Roberto was using his lunch hours and many evenings to make phone calls and set up meetings regarding a host of immigrant rights issues.

In 1977, a call came from Catholic Bishop Gilberto Chavez, inviting Roberto to head up the San Diego diocese's Spanish-speaking evangelism program because of his reputation leading the Mexican-American community at his parish. While this position represented a steep drop in pay, it held the potential of combining two of Roberto's loves: reaching out to Latino newcomers and engaging in immigrant civil rights issues. Roberto left Rohr and took on his first job as a full-time organizer.

As part of his training for this new position, Roberto was sent to the Mexican-American Cultural Center in San Antonio, TX. It was a time of theological awakening, highlighting how a commitment to Christ and a passion for justice were inextricably linked. Noted liberation theologian Gustavo Gutiérrez was brought from Latin America to teach, and Roberto listened as he argued for interpreting the gospel through the eyes of the poor. "See, analyze, and act," intoned Gutiérrez, advocating theological reflection from the standpoint of solidarity with the marginalized and joining them in their struggle against oppression. All this was a revelation for Roberto, and those precious weeks of study enabled him to define and frame his own organizing work in a way that made sense. As he listened to Gutiérrez speak, he felt a growing passion for those suffering abuse under the immigration and law enforcement system.

Roberto returned to San Diego with grand dreams and quickly partnered with some local nuns to organize "Christian Base Communities." These groups studied liberation theology and scripture from the standpoint of their own social experience. This, along with his work combating police and Border Patrol abuses, would gradually provoke the consternation of conservative bishops in the area. They encouraged him to focus his educational efforts around the basics of the Catholic catechism, not on politics and civic engagement. After five years working for the diocese, Roberto was told in 1982 that he could not do both social justice work and church work at the same time. Refusing to abandon the former, Roberto's contract was brought to an abrupt end, forcing him to find a new way to earn a living.

A few months later, Roberto was offered the position of program director for the American Friends Service Committee's (AFSC) U.S.-Mexico Program. At the time the program entailed modest efforts to draw attention to the living conditions of migrant workers and to address economic imbalances between the two countries. Soon after Roberto's arrival, he gave it a new name: the "U.S.-Mexico Border Program," and re-focused its agenda on one ambitious task: addressing human rights issues along the increasingly militarized border.

"Ningun ser humano es ilegal" ("No Human Being Is Illegal")

Over the next two decades, Roberto refused to let the humanity of any person be forgotten. "Law enforcement agencies along the border see the immigrants as nameless and faceless, and that is why it is easy to shoot one—it's just another 'illegal,'" he would say. "So over the years, we have tried to put a human face on the immigration and human rights issue." If someone died along the border, Roberto insisted the death be recorded and that the name and available details of that person's life be publicized. If someone was denied human rights or treated inhumanely by the authorities, Roberto would stubbornly defend his or her humanity. "Blessed are those who mourn," said Jesus (Mt 5:4), and Roberto's work endeavored to mourn the loss of life and dignity that was a casualty of the war at the border where a rich and poor country collide.

The first year with AFSC Roberto worked out of his home, then moved into an office in National City in 1983. It was a time when, as Roberto puts it, "National City was going crazy. Police were arresting everyone that looked Mexican, handing them to the Border Patrol. I was getting a lot of complaints, and was doing as much police abuse work as I was immigration and border work." One recurring grievance he heard was when police were called to investigate a crime in someone's house such as burglary or domestic violence. The first thing they would do upon arrival was to ask residents, if they happen to look Latin American, for their citizenship papers. The police would thus treat people who had called in the crime as suspects, even detaining them if they were unable to prove their citizenship, thereby acting as Immigration and Naturalization Service agents rather than as police. Roberto spent years working with the police, the American Civil Liberties Union, and other civil rights organizations to develop new policies for police. It culminated in 1986 with an official policy stating that only when individuals were in the commission of a crime could police detain them for being undocumented. This was a major victory resulting from countless hours of work, though Roberto noted that the police do not always hold to their policy.

Meanwhile, along the border migrants were getting shot by police and Border Patrol. In response, Roberto held press conferences to denounce the killings as suspicious and pushed for stricter oversight of the police and Border Patrol units involved. Hate crimes were occurring elsewhere in San Diego County as well. For example, groups of young kids with automatic rifles were driving pickups and shooting at migrants along roads in Carlsbad and Escondido, and had gunned down as many as four at a time. Refusing to let such crimes go unaccounted for, Roberto rigorously filed complaints, alerted the press, testified at hearings, and did everything he could to get the police to look into such killings. This work earned Roberto death threats from groups like the White Aryan Resistance, who left swastikas at his door. Roberto figured if someone really wanted to hurt him, there was little he could do to stop them. So he persevered.

In the wake of the Immigration Reform and Control Act of 1986, Roberto helped AFSC fashion a response of noncompliance with the employers' sanctions aspect of the law. The organization refused to fill out the I-9 requirements in hiring staff, and did so publicly. He was at the same time organizing Quakers to provide material aid to farmworkers in north San Diego County as well as advocating for better housing out of a part-time office at Mission San Luis Rey. A few years later Roberto helped reorganize the Centro de Asuntos Migratorios, a full-service legalization clinic in San Diego. There were few aspects of immigrant justice that he did not have a hand in.

In 1994, Roberto found an unwelcome but urgent new task: documenting the skyrocketing deaths of migrants attempting to cross the border. Operation Gatekeeper was launched that year as a national effort to clamp down on illegal immigration along the highly trafficked westernmost section of the border, reaching from the Pacific Ocean to the mountains east of San Diego. Gatekeeper militarized this stretch, with ten-foot-high steel walls, long sections of secondary and tertiary fences, heat sensors, electronic vision detection devices, Black Hawk helicopters patrolling, and thousands of additional Border Patrol agents (Chacon and Davis 2006, 204). It did not, however, prevent those desperate for their survival from attempting to cross the border; it simply shifted the crossing points eastward to mountainous and remote desert terrain, exposing migrants to extremes of heat and cold and leading to a dramatic rise in deaths. As the toll rose, Roberto noticed that no one was keeping careful track of those who were dying and felt this humanitarian crisis needed to be made known.

Recognizing immediately that a coalition of groups would be necessary to document the deaths accurately, Roberto began talking to other human rights organizations on both sides of the border and set up a communications network so that information could be shared. He connected with groups in Tijuana like the Binational Center for Human Rights and Casa de Migrantes, and got cooperation from the Mexican consulate and law enforcement. With the AFSC national office Roberto helped launch the Immigration Law Enforcement Monitoring Project (ILEMP), with groups set up along the border from California to Texas, including San Diego, Tucson, El Paso, Laredo, and Brownsville. ILEMP designed a process and forms for documenting deaths and human rights abuses, and compiled a database in Houston. Data was summarized and interpreted in comprehensive human rights reports, which Roberto and his colleague Maria Jimenez would share in testimonies before congressional committees, at press conferences, and at public rallies.

Prior to October 1994, Roberto and others had documented twenty-four deaths at most in any given year. From 1994 through 2001, 670 deaths were documented in California alone, an extraordinary human rights tragedy. Roberto used this information to argue that Operation Gatekeeper and militarized border operations should be halted, pointing out both the extraordinary human cost and the failure of such operations to accomplish their stated purpose of decreasing illegal immigration. As Roberto emphasized repeatedly, people trying to survive deprivation will risk even the dangers of remote desert lands to make it to the United States. He vividly recalled a conversation in Tijuana with migrants from Mexicali, some as young as ten years old. All had traversed the deserts only to be caught and sent back to Mexico by the Border Patrol. As Roberto listened to them planning another attempt, he asked them if they were aware of the immense risks associated with such a desert crossing: snakes, dehydration, thieves, and brutal heat and cold. They replied matter-of-factly, "We know, but there is no work at home, and we have to feed our families."

In the late 1990s, Roberto helped organize the March for Justice, which was the largest Hispanic civil rights march ever held in the United States. It called for a seven-point agenda, including continuing affirmative action programs, a $7/hour minimum wage, an expanded amnesty program for undocumented immigrants, and more public health services. Roberto was a believer in the power of numbers and the importance of coming together in public protest as another way to draw attention to violence in the borderlands. He had helped organize earlier marches such as the 1986 March for Peace and Justice, which brought together more than 2,000 people from California, Arizona, Texas, and New Mexico to walk to the border at San Ysidro. And he helped with another major demonstration on May 1, 2006, which drew more than a million participants. "We are America," read many banners, sending a message that immigrants are an integral part of America's population, economy, and identity.

Perhaps the most significant demonstration Roberto organized, however, was the faith-rooted "*Posada sin Fronteras*" (see Chapter 9). This Advent liturgy remembers Joseph and Mary's quest for "room at the inn," and Roberto pointed out that this biblical drama was reenacted each day at a border inhospitable to undocumented immigrants. Inaugurated in 1994, the *Posada* has been held annually ever since at Border Field State Park, drawing more than three hundred participants on both sides of the border in 2008.

While justice work captured Roberto's passion and imagination, the challenges he faced were formidable. Not only did he receive death threats and bomb scares, but the wear and tear took a toll on his family life. He attributes the breakup of his first marriage in part to demands of both time and travel, as the work took him to conferences, meetings, and events all over the nation. Following this painful divorce in 1982, Roberto met Yolando Moreno, who was working as an immigration counselor at Chicano Federation of San Diego County. They found a shared concern for the plight of immigrants *and* a romantic relationship that culminated in marriage in 1983. Roberto did not encourage his nine children and twenty-three grandchildren to take up full-time organizing work, recognizing acutely the toll it can take on family life. But he taught them to be socially involved and aware citizens, and was grateful for their patience with and support of his passion.

In 1992, Roberto became the first U.S. citizen to be honored as an international human rights monitor by Human Rights Watch. He later received the prestigious *Ohtli* Award from the Mexican government, the highest honor granted to a non-Mexican national for service to Mexicans abroad. He was also recognized with the *Quezalcoatl* Award, presented to him by the Mexican National Commission for Human Rights. In 2001, Roberto retired after eighteen years of service with the AFSC because of complications with diabetes. He continued to consult with human rights work at the border until he passed away in May 2009, at age seventy-two. One of his last requests was for those attending his funeral mass to wear white, commemorating immigrants who have died trying to cross the border, and the 2006 marches for immigrant rights at which participants dressed in white.

Roberto remains largely unknown to the broader public because of his genuine humility and his refusal to seek the limelight or to engage in political spectacle (though Yolanda did receive a letter of condolence at his death from President Obama). Yet for those in the immigrant rights community, Roberto is nothing short of a hero, a model of gentle ferocity in the cause of justice. He found particular satisfaction in how his efforts paved the way for younger activists, laid the groundwork for policy changes, and contributed to the growth of Latino political power. But it was gospel convictions that "no human being is illegal" or without dignity that lay at the core of his motivation, however private he was about his faith. Those who knew him understood how deeply he had encountered Christ in the guise of the immigrant poor. ¡*Presente!*

Afterword

"Do This in Memory of Me": A Family Story

Ched Myers

"They seemed happy when they were here."

Felix stares out at Santa Rosa Island. We are sitting on ocean-smoothed boulders on the point at El Capitan State Beach. Only here do we break the unspoken taboo against talking about our fathers.

When we were young our families used to camp along this magical coastline, where rolling hills of chaparral embrace the kelp-braided waters of the Santa Barbara Channel. From here you can sometimes see Point Conception, which the indigenous Chumash called *Humqaq*, the "Western Gate," where departed spirits went to *Similaqas*, the other world. Felix and I have decided that the spirits of our fathers must linger around here, too, sitting around some ghostly campfire drinking too much as they did, spinning jokes late into the night, the roar of laughter keeping us awake.

I reach for a piece of driftwood and turn it around in my hands, thinking of the only time my father and I ever went camping together by ourselves. It was in 1970, four hundred miles down this same coast in Baja, CA. The previous year our family trip to San Quentin had been something of a fiasco. We spent most of a day by the side of a dirt road, trying to stave off sun and dust and despair, our VW bus slumped there like a beached whale, until Dad finally tinkered the engine back to life. After that, the rest of the family decided they'd had their fill of off-road adventures in Baja's rugged desert lands, so the next year it was just Dad and me.

I close my eyes and see the photograph on my memorial wall at home. His hat is tipped back, his foot propped against a rock, in his hand held out toward me a cup of *pulpo en su tinta* ("octopus in its own ink"). We had stopped at *La Bufadora* on our way south from Ensenada, and he'd purchased the *pulpo* from a sleepy vendor. He topped it with slightly sour *salsa picante* and put out the fire with cold beer. He had a mustache at the time, and he looks at ease with his *mestizaje*. Here he could eat all the tortillas he wanted, belt out off-key strains of *"La Adelita,"* oil his rusty Spanish. Like the memories it evokes, the picture seems to orbit around his smile.

★   ★   ★

The maternal side of Dad's family were all *Californios* (Mexican Californians), a patrimony that both delights and haunts me. It seems to me now that most of the time Dad's *raza* was buried deep under the surface of his assimilated suburban persona, mothballed beneath Republican politics and a corporate wardrobe, exiled like a bastard son. Sobered by the hard catechism of growing up half-Chicano and poor, my father had, like California itself, succumbed to the imposed "American dream," conforming to its dictates and internalizing its delusions. As kids we saw only glimpses of his flickering *mestizaje*: in his love for tamales, for example, or how his car radio was always set to KWKW so he could listen to the Dodger ballgames in Spanish on his solitary commute home from downtown Los Angeles.

When I was young he used to invite all my friends in for dinner without warning, to my mother's distress. The famous hospitality of *Californios* was roundly maligned by ambitious nineteenth-century Yankee colonists. "These people are friendly to a fault," wrote Richard Henry Dana contemptuously, "and love nothing so much as a *fandango* or *rodeo*. They lack the industry and thrift to tame this place for commerce."

However assimilated, Dad's smile would betray the spirit in his bones, and I lived for it. It was the first thing I saw when I stepped off the plane, returning from a dark and difficult high school year abroad in Scandinavia. That was an embrace warmer than the Prodigal's father's robe, richer than the fatted calf, promising a hearth in what had become for me an increasingly alienating world. And his smile is what I recall of the last time I saw him before his hospitalization. The first Gulf War was raging, about which we disagreed profoundly. Just as we felt the argument coming on, he mercifully changed the subject by bringing out an old cache of photographs of his "anseesters." We spent the evening poring together over them and talked of taking a trip to the Azores to trace the roots of his great *abuelo* Mendosa. A week later U.S. flyboys were on a turkey shoot in Iraq, and my dad was dead.

At the memorial service, my mom asked me to preach on John 14:2. "There was always lots of room in my father's house," I began. Then my grief welled up, and I couldn't go on for a full two minutes.

★   ★   ★

The political winds of imperial conquest and settlement, and the global economic currents of boom and bust, push and pull people like great tides. They have shaped and re-shaped the shorelines of countries and cultures since the first soldiers of fortune landed lost on the beaches of Great Turtle Island. To blame the immigrant for the tides is like blaming a fallen apple for gravity.

Who is legal, who is an immigrant, and even who is native ebbs and flows with these tides. Five generations ago in California, it was Anglo trappers and fortune hunters who were sneaking into Mexican territory as undocumented "explorers." But they were well schooled by two centuries of westward American expansion on the profitability of squatting and expropriation. In 1846, on the eve of the Mexican–American War, Yankee settlers used cunning planning and positioning to launch an almost bloodless coup that paved the way for the American occupation of California and, four years later, statehood. *Californio* general Mariano Guadalupe Vallejo recognized at that time the rising tide of imperial inevitability that was reaching inexorably from "sea to shining sea." (Katharine Lee Bates' famous line from her 1893 song "America the Beautiful" was only echoing Thomas Jefferson's vision of a century earlier.)

My great, great grandfather Francisco Mendosa was probably already here when the Treaty of Guadalupe Hidalgo ceded California to the United States in 1848. He had settled in Sonora, so named because Mexican gold miners were congregated (and segregated) there. Pushed to the New World by the tide of European revolutions that year, he escaped from Portugal to Veracruz, Mexico, then came north by sea. My elderly mother still has the sturdy embossed leather sea chest that, according to (typically unverifiable) family tradition, had carried Mendosa's belongings.

Mendosa married Ynez Nuñez, who was born in Mexico in 1829 (despite exhaustive genealogical research, we've found no prior family records). Apparently he didn't do well in the gold fields; census data from the 1850s list Mendosa as a "gardner." Ynez' second daughter, Maria Rosario, married Louis Guerena, a saloon keeper; she was later active in the Native Daughters of the Golden West. Their daughter Ynez Belle was my grandmother. One tantalizing old photo shows her as a child standing next to an unidentified native woman in front of a tent or tepee; there is no explanation on the back.

Economic tides swirled my grandmother from foothill Sonora to urban San Francisco, where she and Edward Myers, a German American tire salesman, endured the hard times of the Depression. As a boy, my dad shared a room with his *abuela* Maria, who still spoke mostly Spanish. After the early death of her husband, Ynez followed my dad down to Los Angeles, where he supported her in a small apartment. She knew almost no one and felt out of place, sitting uncomfortably during family gatherings at the elegant home of my mother's parents, who were managerial class and thoroughly WASP.

"Gama" Ynez was a devout Catholic, which seemed bizarre to us five kids, since Dad, though an altar boy in his youth, had long ago bailed from the church. She seemed depressed and grumpy most of the time and never spoke of the past to us. Then again, we never asked. Why would a suburban adolescent, preoccupied with baseball and his neighborhood lawn-mowing franchise, be interested in a fading *Californio* legacy? I could kick myself.

*   *   *

One of my most treasured possessions is a little leather *bolsita* I discovered tucked away in my dad's bureau. In it were two Spanish coins: a two *reales* copper dated 1852, and a five *centimes* from 1870. When I inquired, my mom related the family story, presumably passed on by Gama, perhaps after a rare drink: the purse had allegedly been given to her grandmother Ynez by the famous *Californio bandido* Joaquin Murietta.

According to tradition—a mix of foggy history and heroic legend—Murietta was a Mexican miner beaten by Yankees in the goldfields, who then raped his wife. Thereafter he roamed all over the state, famously robbing *gringos* and distributing the proceeds to disinherited *Californios*, a bona fide Golden State Robin Hood. To officials of the newly minted state of California, of course, Murietta was just a notorious horse thief and "terrorist," and in 1853 Rangers were recruited to track him down. They claimed to have killed him that summer around Pacheco Pass in northern California; as proof, they circulated a head pickled in a jar of alcohol so they could collect their bounty. A quarter-century later, a certain O. P. Stidger went on record that he'd heard Murietta's sister say the head was not her brother's. Soon after, numerous sightings of old man Murrieta were reported; the preserved head, meanwhile, was destroyed in the 1906 San Francisco earthquake. It was just enough to leave the door ajar for the legend to live on.

After poking around, I discovered that many old *Californio* families have similar tales of something *they* received from Murietta. I could take this to mean that the tale of my *bolsita* was mere nineteenth-century fabulation. But I choose not to so dismiss this mysterious yet palpable talisman; it is, after all, one of the few remnants from the Mendosa clan's paltry material legacy. I prefer an alternative, if ethnographic, interpretation: these sorts of family stories exemplify the popular mythologies that preserve suppressed truths of history's underside.

After all, *Californios* were systematically disinherited of land and influence during the first decades of American rule, and "social banditry" was a common response. "My anseestors shoulda stole land rather than horses," my dad once intoned ruefully and only half in jest when his lone real estate investment went sour. But the social history of Mexican California was absent from our public school curricula and even more effectively obfuscated by the twentieth-century entertainment industry. The Murietta myth was reworked into the popular and romantic "Zorro" serials of pulp novels and Disney movies, in which the hero was a decidedly genteel rascal of the landed class and the villains the Mexican colonial rulers of California. Ah, but how I loved watching those shows as a kid! An old photo captures me at six, costumed as Zorro for Halloween.

The Ventura River watershed where we now live and work was still predominately Mexican up until the discovery of oil in the 1870s, and the *bandido famoso* allegedly retreated in the local foothills of the Santa Ynez Mountains. Today I can see Murietta Peak from my study window, and we often hike the nearby Murietta Trail. I enjoy imagining him camped out in one of the surviving (and still remote) oak groves. But the trail of my ancestors has run cold. My dad was frustrated in his attempts to reconstruct his family story, defeated by lost or destroyed records. He was an only child, and everyone from the *Californio* side is now long gone. This is how it is in America: our immigrant identities are invariably fractured, dispersed by the incessant tides of imperial history and its discontents. All the more reason, then, to cling to the fragments that remain, reading them like potsherds. Like Gama's *bolsita*.

Remember what has been dismembered. This exhortation lies at the heart of the church's eucharistic ritual, repeated with each element for emphasis. It reiterates and sums up the deep wisdom of biblical faith, the product of a people all too familiar with distress, displacement, and near disappearance. *Whenever you ingest this memory*, said Jesus on the eve of his execution, *you join yourselves to our historic struggle to make the broken body whole*. It was, and is, both invitation and imperative, equally personal and political. If we refuse to heed it, we are doomed to drift forever on or be drowned by the tides of empire, refugees all.

★   ★   ★

"Let's go catch the sunset," says Felix, and we begin walking back around El Capitan point.

"Ever eaten *pulpo en su tinta*?" I ask him. He stops and looks at me nonplussed. "Tastes like shit," I laugh, blinking back tears. And there's my dad, smiling, holding the cup toward me.

"But as far as I'm concerned," I add after a moment, "it's the body and blood."

Appendix 1

Current Contours of Immigration Policy Reform

Allison Johnson

Addressing the fact that immigration policy is a complex and challenging issue for the United States, President Barack Obama has stated, "America is a nation of immigrants and a nation of laws." Between these two identities lies the contentious political issue of immigration reform.

The vast majority of Americans acknowledge that the current immigration system is not working. Elected officials, however, have yet to bring forward practical solutions to bring about reform. But while politicians fret over the electoral consequences of supporting or opposing hot-button measures, the lives and livelihoods of some ten to twelve million undocumented immigrants currently in the country hang in the balance. Families are waiting to be reunited with loved ones, and unscrupulous business owners are exploiting immigrant labor for their own profit. These questions affect urban centers, border communities, and small towns across the nation. Immigration reform, often touted as the pariah of modern American politics, must be confronted head on if this nation is to respect and continue its immigrant history.

Over the past decade, immigrants and advocates have been strategizing, lobbying, and educating about the need for a *comprehensive* federal approach to immigration reform. Since 2006 it has been widely acknowledged in the public conversation that in order to address the underlying problems within the current system, reform cannot be accomplished through a series of separate bills. Comprehensive reform, however, requires a multifaceted approach with many interconnected pieces, each of which has its own political baggage, history, and constraints (see Immigration Policy Center 2009). Issues include the future flow of workers, family immigration and reunification, detention reform, legalization for the undocumented, border security, immigrant integration and naturalization.

Strategists believe that with broad-based support from allies in the business, labor, law enforcement, and faith-based and immigrant advocacy communities, enough political power could be exercised to move comprehensive immigration reform through Congress. While this holistic approach has not yet resulted in a change to the law, it is still considered the preferred method of moving forward among congressional analysts.

Several core elements of reform are widely agreed upon by proponents and politicians alike, although parties differ about priorities. For example, it is generally acknowledged that it is both immoral and impractical to order mass deportation of the millions of current undocumented residents; on the other hand, the security of U.S. residents depends upon knowing who is here. Thus a legalization program must be part of reform, so people will come out of the shadows and register in exchange for temporary work authorization. The pathway to legalization and eventual citizenship should be practical and fair, requiring criminal background checks to weed out those who threaten the safety of our communities. By legalizing the broadest number of eligible immigrants already in the United States, millions of hardworking individuals will be brought into the mainstream and contribute even more so to the economic and cultural life of the United States.

Another significant aspect of the immigration debate concerns the role and authority of immigration enforcement agencies, both on the border and in the interior. Since September 11, 2001, both major political parties have framed the immigration debate in terms of national security. Advocates for stricter control measures focus on the U.S.-Mexico border and call for "security first" measures such as fencing, walls, electronic surveillance, and even a sustained military presence along significant sections of the border in order to deter and stop the flow of undocumented workers. Border community coalitions, in contrast, have spoken out strongly against the assumption that the border is an inherently violent region that needs militarization in order to restore law and order.

Those who advocate for stricter control of the southern border tend to ignore the economic push and pull factors driving undocumented immigration as well as the inherent inequality between the United States and its neighbors to the south. If the United States cannot meet its demand for labor or create safe channels for legal workers to enter, people seeking opportunity will continue to find a way to cross the border out of desperation and economic necessity. There is still too much truth to the adage that our border posts two contradictory signs: "Help Wanted" and "Keep Out." Policies must thus be predicated upon a proper analysis of root causes of migration. Moreover, practical and effective border enforcement tools and technologies should focus on drug cartels and human traffickers, not potential painters or nannies.

Still, border security as the primary means to solve illegal migration has dominated the conversation in Washington in recent years. The harshest proenforcement and anti-immigrant rhetoric often comes from congressional representatives from interior states such as Oklahoma, Iowa, Georgia, and Nebraska. Such states do not experience issues related to the borderlands, but they are experiencing the changing face of America. Rural communities across America in the heartland are having to face the realities of an aging workforce and the exodus of young, educated professionals from small towns to urban centers. Immigrants, in turn, are increasingly filling the voids in farming and other traditional industries based in rural America. In northwest Iowa, for example, meatpacking factories would have closed their doors long ago if it had not been for waves of Mexican and Central American immigrants. As these families settle in, create new businesses, and invest in community life, rural America is seeing dramatic demographic change, which affects how older residents perceive immigration issues. With census projections indicating that the United States may become a "majority-minority" country by 2042 (see Roberts 2008), the declining dominant group's anxieties over immigrant integration, cultural differences, and American identity are unavoidable and will continue to play a major role in politics.

But the future of American politics is being influenced by the current experiences of injustice. Legal immigrant children are seeing their families torn apart, and undocumented youth are being denied their dreams of opportunity and employment in the only country they've ever known because they don't possess a Social Security number. Thus the earliest impressions of democracy among a whole immigrant generation are being tainted with injustice and suffering. We all have a stake, therefore, in facing the challenges of fair and comprehensive immigration reform. The question is no longer whether the nation should address these challenges head on, but rather how much longer we can wait without significant action from the federal government.

People of faith must respond to this historic moment, and to the biblical mandates articulated in this volume. We must advocate for immigration policies that uphold values of dignity, compassion, and justice. As people who answer to a higher authority than the government, we have an important voice to exercise in the current debate. In particular, churches can speak eloquently and specifically about the impact of our broken immigration system on families. Immigrants often turn to churches as places of refuge and restoration in the midst of their struggle, and thus church leaders and providers deal directly with the practical and spiritual challenges that immigrant families face "on the ground." When a mother is pulled over for a traffic violation, only to land in jail because of an immigration violation, who will pick up her child from daycare? Who will support a family when its primary breadwinner is deported? Communities of faith are often first responders to such crises, and these stories of hardship must be shared with those in the position to make real policy changes that will support, not undermine, the value of family.

The religious community is also uniquely positioned to serve as a bridge across differences on immigration and a source of healing and reconciliation. With the rise of fear-based legislation at the state level, immigration has become a local issue. Anti-immigrant rhetoric, which is often difficult to distinguish from hate speech, is ubiquitous. People of faith can speak out against such rhetoric, and the inevitably accompanying hate crimes, with moral authority. Regardless of where one stands on the politics of the issue, the dehumanization of immigrants is at clear odds with Christian values of compassion, mercy, and dignity. As false information and scapegoating myths about immigrants continue to circulate on cable news networks, talk radio, and the blogosphere, it is the church's responsibility to promote a deeper conversation that moves past rhetoric and forward to common ground.

As the essays in this volume argue repeatedly, the most significant element Christians can bring to the immigration debate is our roots in biblical and our own migrant history. God's people have always been on the move and on the margins. We follow a refugee Christ whose family fled to Egypt to escape political persecution and who had no place to lay his head (see Chapter 3). Our primary identities are not determined by stamps on a passport because we ultimately belong to the kingdom of heaven, in which there are no borders or limitations on love and justice.

Appendix 2

Recovering Our Cultural History

Ched Myers

In the Introduction I asserted that "as a pastoral task it could not be more important for churches to help their members work through their conflicted identities as immigrant peoples." And in Chapter 3 I touched upon the psychic legacy of what Chellis Glendinning and Donna Awatere have described as the "original trauma" of immigrant displacement (I have explored this in some depth in Myers 1994, 132–39). An essential step in becoming an ally in the work of immigrant justice is to engage in critical reflection on our own immigrant stories and identities. In order to clearly see and respond to current immigrant realities, we must *remember* our own *dismembered* pasts, and *revise* our own *devised* narratives concerning family, ethnicity, and nation.

The following simple workshop (or personal exercise) was originally developed by a team of popular educators as part of a study process for *Pax Christi* during the 1992 Columbus Quincentenary (see Taylor et al. 1992, 71f; the paragraphs below are significantly edited and updated). Its purpose is to better understand the social and historical context of our own immigrant experiences, to identify any trauma and/or dissociation generated by this history, and to reintegrate this truth into our personal and political understanding of immigrant legacies and current realities.

1. *Genealogy.* Prepare a genogram of your family history back to the immigrant generation(s) if possible. Explanations and templates are available online (e.g., http://www.genopro.com/genogram/templates/). The further back the immigrant generation(s), the more lines you'll have to work on. It is common to have uneven information about the various ancestral lines. A shorter version of this exercise is to trace only one line, preferably one that interests you most.

2. *Geography.* Draw a map of the world. Don't worry about your artistic talent. Mark on the map the country or countries where your family originated. Note any particular information you have about the economic status, religious and political beliefs, and cultural values of your ancestors in the Old World.

   a. If your family is indigenous, note what part of this continent they live(d) in, and describe what you know about their circumstances at the time of first contact with Europeans.

   b. If your family emigrated to the Americas, what were the circumstances in their countries of origin and in the world at the time(s) of emigration?

3. *Immigration.* If your family emigrated to the Americas, indicate on the map what you know about your family's journey here, including when and how they came, and why. Were these movements voluntary? Was the journey dangerous?

What do you know about the "push" and "pull" factors in their emigration?

4. *Arrival: Place and People.* Who inhabited the land(s) your family or ethnic community settled before they arrived? What do you know about the culture and life of these indigenous inhabitants? Did your immigrant people interact, fight, displace, or intermarry with them? What happened to these indigenous people, and how did your cultural history impact theirs? What other ethnic groups were in the area(s) your family settled in, and what were relations with them?

5. *Socioeconomic Circumstances.* What happened to your family's immigrant generation(s) upon arrival in the New World socially and economically? Did they experience discrimination, homelessness, and/or marginalization? How was land or a home procured, if at all? What strategies of accommodation or resistance were employed? How was wealth accumulated or poverty perpetuated over subsequent generations, and what were patterns of upward or downward mobility? What senses of status, entitlement, or inferiority were passed on? How did war or slavery impact your family? What were gender patterns, and how did they change over time? How did all these factors contribute to fracturing, or keeping intact, the extended family?

6. *Cultural Traditions.* What cultural traditions did your immigrant ancestors bring (food, language, dress, music, social organization, religious expression, etc.)? For how many generations did differ-

ent traditions survive, and what were the factors involved in their atrophy? What fragments remain to you, and how were they passed on in your upbringing and your own family? At what point was the immigrant identity lost in your family line, or if maintained, how? How was assimilation promoted or lamented in your family?

7. *Gaps in the History.* If some or all of your family history is not available to you, why not? How was it lost or compromised, or who refused to talk? What role do unverifiable family "legends" play in the stories you received or have recovered? How do these silences make you feel, and what does it mean for your own sense of identity if some or all of these stories have been lost or silenced? Are there resources that you could draw on if you wanted to know more about your family and/or ethnic group history?

8. *Your Story: Place and People.* Where did *you* grow up, and what other racial and ethnic groups resided there? How were relations between and among the groups? What do you know about their work, community life, customs, religious traditions, culture, and values? How did your family view itself in relation to these other groups and to the society at large, and how did race, class, and gender shape your upbringing? How many different geographic locations did you reside in growing up, and how has this affected your sense of place and identity?

9. *Social Power.* Discuss your experiences as a person *having* or *lacking* power in relation to the following

aspects of identity: racial, ethnic, class, gender, sexual, and professional. Where did your privilege(s) or lack of privilege(s) come from? Reflect for a moment on an experience in which you knew yourself to be the oppressor in a specific personal or social situation (either by excluding or by dominating another human being). What was going on for you in that moment, and how did it impact your perception of the other? Now reflect on a moment when you have personally experienced oppression, marginalization, or invisibility.

10. *Economics.* What is your experience with poverty? Have you or anyone in your family ever been poor? How do you define poverty? What are your attitudes toward the poor, middle class, the rich? How are these experiences and attitudes related to your family's immigrant history?

11. *Religion.* With which community(ies) of faith has your family been associated? What were the most important values that this community taught you? Reflect on a time in your life when your own faith journey departed in significant ways from the tradition(s) with which your family identified. From your perspective now, which of those values taught by your faith community contribute to social transformation and which do not? What values do you think are most needed today, especially as they relate to immigrant justice?

12. *American Identity.* What have you been taught about what it means to be an American? Who taught you this? How would you define the "American dream?" To what degree would you

say this "dream" shapes your aspirations for the future? How have you become disillusioned with these narratives? Is "America" synonymous with the United States in your mind? What is your current experience with immigrants? Are they positive or negative, and why? What might you do to learn more about the realities faced by poorer and undocumented immigrants?

Notes

Introduction

[1] These include: Ben Daniel, *Neighbor: Christian Encounters with "Illegal" Immigration* (2010); Gemma Talud Cruz, *An Intercultural Theology of Migration: Pilgrims in the Wilderness—Studies in Systematic Theology* (2010); Miguel De La Torre, *Trails of Hope and Terror: Testimonies on Immigration* (2009); Donald Kerwin, *And You Welcomed Me: Migration and Catholic Social Teaching* (2009); Matt Soerens and Jenny Hwang, *Welcoming the Stranger: Justice, Compassion & Truth in the Immigration Debate* (2009); Daniel Carroll, *Christians at the Border: Immigration, the Church, and the Bible* (2008); and Daniel Groody and Gioacchino Campese, eds., *A Promised Land, A Perilous Journey: Theological Perspectives on Migration* (2008). See also Maruskin (2004).

[2] Elaine Enns and I used a similar format in our recent two-volume study of the theology and practices of restorative justice (Myers and Enns 2009).

[3] In fact Jesus was alluding to the Deuteronomic tradition of Sabbath year debt-release (Dt 15:1–18). Far from legitimating poverty, this legislation was intended as a hedge against the tendency of human societies to stratify power and wealth in ways that created permanent underclasses. If periodic debt-amnesty was practiced, "There will be no one in need among you" (Dt 15:4). But the practical Deuteronomist anticipated rightly that people would forever be equivocating on the demands of social justice so that, lamentably, "there will never cease to be needy ones in your land." Thus vigilant compassion is the plumb line of the law: "I command you: Open your hand to the poor" (Dt 15:11). It is *this* tradition that Jesus is appealing to in Mark 14:7.

[4] Another, even more sinister, byproduct of these forces is human trafficking; although we do not tackle this issue here, much of our analysis applies to it as well. See Bales (2004).

Chapter 3

¹ See http://nobelprize.org/nobel_prizes/peace/laureates/1992/tum-bio.html; Menchu (1984).

² On the Sanctuary Movement of the 1980s, see Crittendon (1988), Coutin (1993), and Cunningham (1995).

³ For information on the New Sanctuary Movement, see http://www.newsanctuarymovement.org and http://www.religionlink.com/tip_081208.php.

⁴ For example, Pu'uhonua O Honaunau, a national park on the big island of Hawai'i, is the site of a precontact indigenous "city of refuge," which, as in Torah, provided sanctuary for unconvicted man slaughterers.

⁵ The Hebrew noun *ger* appears some ninety-two times (and the verb *gur* ninety-four times) in the Hebrew Bible, usually referring to "sojourners" or "resident aliens" in the land. Sometimes it describes the Hebrews as strangers in another land, other times strangers in the land of Israel.

⁶ For alternative feminist-critical readings of Judges 19, see, e.g., Scholz (2010) and Trible, who argues that this story and Genesis 19 "show that rules of hospitality in Israel protect only males" (1984, 75). Trible's detailed and compelling interpretation of Judges 19–21 has been highly influential in its focus on misogyny; I contend here that the text can *also* be seen as a parable of the sin of inhospitality.

⁷ Elsewhere in the Hebrew Bible *caph* usually connotes the threshold of the Temple (e.g., 2 Kgs 12:9, 25:18; Is 6:4; Jer 52:24; Ez 43:8).

Chapter 5

¹ "Today" (Gk *sāneron*) is an existential notion of great significance that is used throughout Luke (see, e.g., 2:11, 5:26, 13:32f, 19:5, 9, 23:43, 24:21).

² Isaiah is cited almost six hundred times in the New Testament, far more than any other part of the Hebrew Bible, and seventy-eight times in Luke alone. Luke 4:18–19 follows the Greek text of the Septuagint, with the following exceptions: (1) it omits Isaiah's phrase "soothe the broken-hearted," (2) "sight to the blind" is not in the Hebrew text, and (3) "freeing the oppressed" is from Isaiah 58:6 (the Greek *aphiēmi* is used twice in Luke 4:18).

Chapter 8

[1] Besides the accounts of Coutin (1993), Crittenden (1988), and Cunningham (1995), see the moving novel based on these events by one of those indicted, Demetria Martinez' *Mother Tongue* (1997). The trial papers are online at the University of Arizona, http://www.az-archivesonline.org/xtf/view?docId=ead/uoa/UAMS362.xml&doc.view=print;chunk.id=0.

[2] See Chapter 2; for its continuing work today, see http://www.borderlinks.org. Ufford-Chase went on, like Fife, to become moderator of the Presbyterian Church (U.S.A.), and carries on his mission now at Stony Point Center in New York (http://www.stonypointcenter.org).

References

Bacon, David. *The Children of NAFTA: Labor Wars on the U.S./Mexico Border*. Berkeley: University of California Press, 2004.

Bales, Kevin. *Disposable People: New Slavery in the Global Economy*. Rev. ed. Berkeley: University of California Press, 2004.

Brubaker, Pamela. *Globalization at What Price? Economic Change and Daily Life*. Cleveland, OH: Pilgrim Press, 2007.

Bustamante, Jorge. "If There's a Recession in America, It Must Be Time to Pick on Mexico." *Los Angeles Times*, February 16, 1992, M2.

Cardenal, Ernesto. *The Gospel in Solentiname*. Trans. D. Walsh. Rev. ed. Maryknoll, NY: Orbis Books, 2010.

Carroll, Daniel. *Christians at the Border: Immigration, the Church, and the Bible*. Grand Rapids, MI: Baker Academic, 2008.

Chacon, Justin Akers, and Mike Davis. *No One Is Illegal: Fighting Racism and State Violence on the U.S.-Mexico Border*. Chicago: Haymarket Books, 2006.

Coutin, Susan Bibler. *The Culture of Protest: Religious Activism and the U.S. Sanctuary Movement*. Boulder, CO: Westview Press, 1993.

Crittenden, Ann. *Sanctuary: A Story of American Conscience and the Law in Collision*. New York: Grove Press, 1988.

Cruz, Gemma Talud. *An Intercultural Theology of Migration: Pilgrims in the Wilderness (Studies in Systematic Theology)*. Leiden: Brill Academic Publishers, 2010.

Cunningham, Hilary. *God and Cesar at the Rio Grande*. Minneapolis: University of Minnesota Press, 1995.

Daniel, Ben. *Neighbor: Christian Encounters with "Illegal" Immigration*. Philadelphia: Westminster John Knox Press, 2010.

Danner, Mark. *The Massacre at El Mozote: A Parable of the Cold War*. New York: Vintage Books, 1994.

De LaTorre, Miguel. *Trails of Hope and Terror: Testimonies on Immigration.* Maryknoll, NY: Orbis Books, 2009.

Delgado, Richard, and Jean Stefancic. *Critical White Studies: Looking Behind the Mirror.* Philadelphia: Temple University Press, 1997.

Douglas, Mary. *Purity and Danger: An Analysis of Concepts of Pollution and Taboo.* 2nd ed. London: Routledge & Kegan Paul, 1978.

Eisenberg, Evan. *The Ecology of Eden.* New York: Vintage Books, 1998.

Ekblad, Bob. "El Buen Coyote." In *Liberating Biblical Study: Scholarship, Art, and Action in Honor of the Center and Library for the Bible and Social Justice,* ed. L. Dykstra and C. Myers. Eugene, OR: Wipf and Stock Publishers, 2011, 162–65.

Elizondo, Virgil. *Guadalupe: Mother of the New Creation.* Maryknoll, NY: Orbis Books, 2002.

Ellul, Jacques. *The Meaning of the City.* Grand Rapids, MI: Eerdmans, 1970.

Fanestil, John. "Border Crossing: Communion at Friendship Park." *Christian Century* (125:20), October 7, 2008.

Gaiser, Frederick. "A New Word on Homosexuality? Isaiah 56:1–8 as Case Study." *Word & World* (14:3), 1994, 280ff.

Goodman, Amy. "Rev. John Fife Continues Immigrant Humanitarian Work 25+ Years after Launching Sanctuary Movement." Interview on *Democracy Now,* April 23, 2007. Available at http://www.democracynow.org/2007/4/23/rev_john_fife_continues_immigrant_humanitarian.

Gottwald, Norman. *The Hebrew Bible: A Brief Socio-Literary Introduction.* Minneapolis, MN: Fortress Press, 2009.

Grier, William, and Price Cobbs. *Black Rage.* New York: Basic Books, 1968.

Groody, Daniel, and Gioacchino Campese, eds. *A Promised Land, a Perilous Journey: Theological Perspectives on Migration.* South Bend, IN: University of Notre Dame Press, 2008.

Hammock, Clinton. "Isaiah 56:1–8 and the Redefining of the Restoration of Judean Community," *Biblical Theology Bulletin* (30:2), 2000, 46–57.

Horsley, Richard. *The Liberation of Christmas: The Infancy Narratives in Social Context.* New York: Crossroad, 1989.

Horsley, Richard, ed. *In the Shadow of Empire: Reclaiming the Bible as a History of Faithful Resistance.* Louisville, KY: Westminster John Knox Press, 2008.

Horsley, Richard, and Neil Silberman. *The Message and the Kingdom: How Jesus and Paul Ignited a Revolution and Transformed the Ancient World.* New York: Grosset/Putnam, 1997.

Howard-Brook, Wes. *"Come Out, My People!": God's Call out of Empire in the Bible and Beyond.* Maryknoll, NY: Orbis Books, 2010.

Hyde, Lewis. *The Gift.* 25th ann. ed. New York: Vintage Books, 2007.

Immigration Policy Center. "Breaking Down the Problems: What's Wrong with the Immigration System?" Special Report, Washington, DC, October 2009. Available at http://immigrationpolicy.org/sites/default/files/docs/Problem_Paper_FINAL_102109_0.pdf.

Kerwin, Donald. *And You Welcomed Me: Migration and Catholic Social Teaching.* Lanham, MD: Lexington Books, 2009.

Levinas, Emmanuel. "Cities of Refuge." In *Beyond the Verse: Talmudic Writings and Lectures.* Translated by G. Mole. Bloomington, IN: Indiana University Press, 1994.

Martinez, Demetria. *Mother Tongue.* New York: One World/Ballantine, 1997.

Maruskin, Joan. "The Bible as the Ultimate Immigration Handbook: Written by, for and about Migrants, Immigrants, Refugees and Asylum Seekers." Washington, DC: Church World Service, 2004. Available at http://www.iaumc.org/console/files/oFiles_Library_XZXLCZ/CWS-Joan_MaruskinBibleAsUltimateImmigrationHandbook_2L36EITT.pdf.

McClendon, James. *Biography as Theology: How Life Stories Can Remake Today's Theology.* Eugene, OR: Wipf and Stock Publishers, 2002.

Menchu, Rigoberta. *I, Rigoberta Menchu: An Indian Woman in Guatemala.* Trans. Ann Wright. London: Verso, 1984.

Molina, Ana Amalia Guzman. *The Power of Love: My Experience in a U.S. Immigration Jail.* Trans. Marilu MacCarthy. Washington, DC: Ecumenical Program on Central America and the Caribbean, 2003.

Myers, Ched. *Binding the Strong Man: A Political Reading of Mark's Story of Jesus.* 20th ann. ed. Maryknoll, NY: Orbis Books, 2008.

———. *The Biblical Vision of Sabbath Economics.* Washington, DC: Tell the Word Press, 2001.

———. *Who Will Roll Away the Stone? Discipleship Queries for First World Christians.* Maryknoll, NY: Orbis Books, 1994.

Myers, Ched, and Elaine Enns. *Ambassadors of Reconciliation, Vol. I: New Testament Reflections on Restorative Justice and Peacemaking.* Maryknoll, NY: Orbis Books, 2009.

Nevins, Joseph. *Operation Gatekeeper and Beyond: The War on "Illegals" and the Remaking of the U.S.—Mexico Boundary.* 2nd ed. New York: Routledge, 2010.

Peña, Devon. *The Terror of the Machine: Technology, Work, Gender, and Ecology on the U.S.-Mexico Border (CMAS Border & Migration Studies Series).* Austin: University of Texas Press, 1997.

Peterson, Anna. *Martyrdom & Politics of Religion: Progressive Catholicism in El Salvador's Civil War.* Albany, NY: State University of New York Press, 1996.

Pohl, Christine. *Making Room: Recovering Hospitality as a Christian Tradition.* Grand Rapids, MI: Eerdmans, 1999.

Prior, Michael, CM. *Jesus the Liberator: Nazareth Liberation Theology (Luke 4:16–30).* Sheffield, UK: Sheffield Academic Press, 1995.

Ramsay, W. M. *The Letters to the Seven Churches of Asia.* New York: A.C. Armstrong & Son, 1905.

Ringe, Sharon. *Jesus, Liberation and the Biblical Jubilee.* Philadelphia: Fortress, 1985.

Roberts, Sam. "Minorities in U.S. Set to Become Majority by 2042." *New York Times,* August 8, 2008. http://www.nytimes.com/2008/08/14/world/americas/14iht-census.1.15284537.html.

Salvatierra, Alexia. "'Do Not Neglect to Show Hospitality': Sanctuary and Immigrant Justice." In *Liberating Biblical Study: Scholarship, Art, and Action in Honor of the Center and Library for the Bible and Social Justice,* ed. L. Dykstra and C. Myers. Eugene, OR: Wipf and Stock Publishers, 2011, 213–20.

Sassen, Saskia. *The Mobility of Labor and Capital: A Study in International Investment and Labor Flow.* New York: Cambridge University Press, 1988.

Scholz, Susanne. *Sacred Witness: Rape in the Hebrew Bible.* Minneapolis, MN: Fortress Press, 2010.

Sloan, Robert. *The Favourable Year of the Lord: A Study of Jubilary Theology in the Gospel of Luke.* Austin, TX: Schola Press, 1977.

Soerens, Matt, and Jenny Hwang. *Welcoming the Stranger: Justice, Compassion & Truth in the Immigration Debate.* Downers Grove, IL: IVP Books, 2009.

Taylor, Stuart, Ched Myers, Cindy Moe-Lobeda, and Marie Dennis Grosso. *American Journey, 1492–1992: Call to Conversion.* Eerie, PA: Pax Christi USA, 1992.

Tavante, Marco. *Las Abejas: Pacifist Resistance and Syncretic Identities in a Globalizing Chiapas.* New York: Routledge, 2003.

Trible, Phyllis. *Texts of Terror: Literary-Feminist Readings of Biblical Narratives.* Philadelphia: Fortress Press, 1984.

Ufford-Chase, Rick. "1600 Years of Border History." *Church and Society* (July–August), 2005.

Williams, William Appleman. *Empire as a Way of Life.* New York: Oxford University Press, 1980.

Weinberg, Bill. *Homage to Chiapas: The New Indigenous Struggles in Mexico.* New York: Verso, 2000.

Yoder, John Howard. *The Politics of Jesus.* Rev. ed. Grand Rapids, MI: Eerdmans, 1994.

Zinn, Howard. *A People's History of the United States.* New York: HarperCollins, 1995.

Scripture Index